The Wonder of the Presence
The Presence Series Volume 4

John Hammer

Copyright © 2025 by John Hammer

All rights reserved.

No part of this book may be reproduced in any form or by any electronic or mechanical means, including information storage and retrieval systems, without written permission from the author, except for the use of brief quotations in a book review.

All Scripture quotations, unless otherwise indicated, are taken from the Holy Bible, New International Version®, NIV®. Copyright ©1973, 1978, 1984, 2011 by Biblica, Inc.™ Used by permission of Zondervan. All rights reserved worldwide. www.zondervan.comThe "NIV" and "New International Version" are trademarks registered in the United States Patent and Trademark Office by Biblica, Inc.™

Scriptures marked NKJV is taken from the New King James Version®. Copyright © 1982 by Thomas Nelson. Used by permission. All rights reserved.

Scripture marked KJV are taken from the Holy Bible, King James Version. Public Domain.

Contents

Praise for the Presence Series	vii
Acknowledgments	xi
Foreword	xv
Introduction	xvii
1. Presence Mentors	1
2. Strange Fire	5
3. The Lost Ark	9
4. The Cart and the Curse	13
5. Presence Blessing	17
6. Undignified Reverence	19
7. David's Tabernacle	23
8. The Tent Restored	27
9. David's Dream	31
10. Solomon's Temple	35
11. Revival and Reformation Presence	39
12. From the Temple to the Christ	41
13. From Moses to Jesus to Us	45
14. Corporate Presence	49
15. The Dwelling Plan A	53
16. Living Stones	57
17. Teach Through Singing	61
18. Where it All Began	65
19. Registered in Heaven	67
20. The Bride	69
21. God is Present	73
22. Enthroned	75
23. Restore Us	77
24. Let's Go	79
25. The Commanded Blessing	81
26. Worthless Assemblies	85
27. Noisy Songs	89

28. Walk Humbly	93
29. Windows of Heaven	95
30. Among the Lampstands	99
31. First Love	103
32. The Greatest Commandment	107
33. Pure Joy	109
34. Tarry	111
35. The Kingdom Belongs to the Kids	115
36. The Greatest	117
37. Others and the Altar	121
38. Ask, Seek, Knock	123
39. Presence Deception	127
40. Portraits of the Father	131
41. Don't Give Up	135
42. Mercy for Sinners	137
43. Good to Give Thanks	139
44. The Benefits	141
45. The Upright Shall Dwell	145
46. Thanksgiving Choirs	147
47. Joy Strength	149
48. Adoration Prayer	151
49. His Love Endures Forever	155
50. The Spiritual Discipline of Thanksgiving	159
51. The Sacrifice at the End of Sacrifice	161
52. Who Loves Much?	163
53. Gratitude Miracles	167
54. Multiplication	169
55. Thanksgiving > Anxiety	173
56. Not Contained	177
57. Deny Yourself	179
58. Suffering and Glory	183
59. Overshadowed	187
60. The Grace of His Face	191
61. Build Yourself Up	193
62. Advent	197
63. Incarnation	201
64. The Seed	205

65. Immanuel	209
66. A Child is Born	211
67. The Shoot	215
68. Glory Revealed	219
69. O Little Town of Bethlehem	223
70. Come Away	227
71. Redemption of Our Brokenness	231
72. Costly Christmas	233
73. Light Power	237
74. The Name Jesus	241
75. Overshadowed	245
76. The Forerunner	249
77. Joyful Womb	253
78. Magnificat	257
79. He Has Come	259
80. Peace on Earth	263
81. Dedicated	267
82. Moved by the Spirit	269
83. Hidden Heroes	273
84. Wise Men	277
85. Christmas Eve	279
86. Christmas Day	281
87. In the Same Way	285
88. Present You	289
89. Throne Room Mission	293
90. The Rider on the White Horse	297
91. Eternal Dwelling	301
92. Maranatha	305
Bibliography	309
Also by John Hammer	311
Contact	313
About the Author	315

Praise for the Presence Series

John Hammer's book is a masterful blend of theology, practical wisdom, personal stories, and lived experience. It not only inspires but challenges us to deepen our devotional lives in a way that feels accessible and transformative. This is a must-read for anyone looking to enrich their spiritual journey—I highly recommend it!

Dr. Joseph Mattera
Overseeing Bishop of *Christ to Covenant Coalition*

Love and tremendously appreciate the powerful and unique combination of a great intellect and beautiful heart that Pastor John possesses as a rising kingdom generational leader. This awesome book gives us wonderful insights surrounded by deep, biblically accurate theology. The outcome of reading this will be an increased hunger and deeper understanding of the presence of God.

Dr. Michael Maiden,
Lead pastor *Church for the Nations*, Phoenix, AZ.

John Hammer has written a fantastic series of devotional books that are sure to draw every reader into thoughtful worship, deep conviction, and a faith filled response to God's Word. As I read through each day, I found myself not only encouraged but looking forward to the next topic to ponder. These books are filled with Biblical truth, practical insights, and personal prayers that will help you to walk more closely with the Lord in your everyday life. I wholeheartedly recommend this series of books with great anticipation for how the Lord will use it in your life!

Pastor Ben Dixon
Lead Pastor - *Northwest Church*
Author - *Hearing God and Prophesy*

The Presence 4-part series written by John Hammer does an incredible job at inviting us as followers to not just know about God, but to live a life that is intimate with Him. *The Presence* captures the essence, attributes and beautiful mysteries of Christ, causing us to reflect and embrace our Savior from new depths and perspectives. John sets before us an insightful and thoughtful collection of writings that beg us to stop being busy for Jesus, but to actually know Him and walk with Him daily. In the current state of our world, we can't think of anything more important.

Sean & Christa Smith
Sean & Christa Smith Ministries

My son, John Hammer, has written a devotional on *The Presence* (of the Lord). My wife, Terry, and I used it for our daily devotions for a year. It was such a blessing to our daily walk with the Lord. The devotional was biblical, challenging, refreshing and, most importantly, brought us into His presence. Absorb yourself in it and you will be absorbed in His presence. Remember, Psalm 16 tells us "in His presence is fullness of joy!" Enjoy and enter His Presence as you read!

Dr. Dan C. Hammer
Sonrise Christian Center
Senior Apostolic Leader
Seattle Bible School President

This series of books exploring the presence of God flows from John's heart of love for Jesus. John is a practical teacher with an ability to provoke you to desire Jesus in a deeper and more personal way. I have known John and his wife Grace for decades and have always been inspired by their simple love for Jesus, and their longing to serve Him well. In this season, we are ready to experience more of His presence and power in our lives every day. Let these books teach you how to open the eyes of your heart, and then engage in your walk with Jesus with greater joy, revelation, and authenticity.

Rachel Hickson
Heartcry for Change, Oxford, UK

Pastor John Hammer paints a picture of the beauty of Christ through both inspirational stories and theological truths. The Presence book feels similar to the strength and comfort found in an old friend who carries sound wisdom and holds your arms up when you're weary. It will lift your soul and draw you into the deep places of the Lord's heart! The Presence book is written in a way that will inspire you to hunger for more of Jesus each and every day.

Theo Koulianos Jr
A Place for Family

I have had the privilege of knowing John Hammer for nearly two decades, and I have always been inspired by his profound relationship with the Father. In every conversation, you sense that John is not just a man of knowledge and information, but someone with genuine experience and deep intimacy with the Lord. His writings on the presence of God are a reflection of this life of devotion. They are not mere teachings, but the fruit of years of inheritance and personal practice.
What I love about this book is its accessibility: it is easy to understand and follow for a new believer, yet it offers depth and wisdom for even the most seasoned and mature Christians. I wholeheartedly endorse and recommend this work to anyone seeking to grow in relationship with Jesus and deepen their revelation of Him."

Meesh Fomenko
Evangelist
Be Moved

A Christian cannot pursue Christ and not be in His Presence. His presence is the sustenance needed for a long-lasting Christian life. It is the pursuit of Him and His Word that draws on the presence of God.
In *The Presence*, John Hammer takes readers on a transformative journey into the heart of God's presence. Through vivid storytelling, profound biblical insights, and heartfelt prayers, each devotional invites you to experience the tangible nearness of God in everyday life. With every page, John masterfully intertwines Scripture and personal testimony, making the deep truths of God's love and mercy accessible and practical. This book is a treasure for anyone longing to encounter God more intimately and live with a renewed sense of awe and wonder. A must-read for seekers of His presence.

Paul Martini
Pastor of *New Life City*

Acknowledgments

First of all to all my daily blog readers and those of you who constantly commented and sent notes of encouragement along the journey of daily writing. What a joy you brought to me through your testimonies and personal insights you had along the way. I will always cherish that year of writing and the way it connected me with all of you.

A book can't come together without a great editor, thank you Carolyn for handling the edits but also the layout and process. This book series would have just stayed on the internet as blog posts if it wasn't for your effort and excellence turning it into a book. Thank you!

Mike Lewis, I am grateful for your design and art skills to produce such beautiful art. You brought our vision for arts and exalting Christ together for our church at Sonrise and I am very blessed to get to use some of the other works you produced for this cover art.

Jason, you are a man of many talents. Thank you for your work on the cover design. I appreciate your skillful work and heart to serve.

Jake, your idea to write this as a daily blog sparked something in me that helped bring all of this together. I'm so grateful for you sharing that with me.

Sonrise Christian Center, Elders, staff and members, thank you for being a church that goes after God's presence with all your heart. The past two years have been so incredible as God's manifest presence invades our gatherings. Your prayers, encouragement and support to write has been so wonderfully encouraging.

My family has been my biggest encouragement. My wife, and kids, Hailey, Emma, Justus and Addi all gave me the time to write. My dad and mom read my blog every day and encouraged me all along to make this a book. I'm so thankful for you all.

I'm most thankful for Jesus. Thank you for saving me and sharing Your presence with me. Thank You for carrying me through the darkest moments of my life and revealing Your nearness when I needed You the most.

I dedicate this book to my wife and best friend of 20 years, Grace Elaine. Your love for Jesus, prayers and constant encouragement to me made this work possible. I love you so much!

Foreword

"Come and see," Jesus invited in John 1:39. Eager to start a new life with purpose, John and Andrew are introduced to Jesus by John the Baptist. As they approach, Jesus turns and asks, "What do you want?" They respond by asking Him, "Where do you live? What is home to you?" Jesus replies, "Come and see." This invitation extends to us each day—to be with Jesus, follow Him, become like Him, and learn to live and love as He did.

After years of a busy schedule, I recently graduated with a doctorate. During a season of fatigue, the Holy Spirit whispered, "Leif, hurry is one of love's greatest enemies." It's challenging to be fully present with His presence when we're constantly in a rush. The next invitation was clear: to slow down enough to catch up with God (1 John 4:16 reminds us, "God is love").

Our Heavenly Father calls us to a major upgrade in the quality and depth of our life and ministry. As I daily practice His presence, I was asked to write the foreword for this devotional about experiencing the presence of God. I first met John Hammer in 2004 when Dr. Randy Clark invited me to teach at the first healing school in Seattle. John and I instantly connected as family and friends. Today, Pastor John and his wife, Grace, lead a Kingdom-focused church and movement that transforms lives, impacts regions, and disciples nations. It has been my honor to serve as one of John's spiritual fathers, observing his deep commitment to hosting the presence of Jesus. His journey in sonship and leadership serves as an example of what it means to walk with the Father and love others, defining the promised land God calls us to occupy. John's passionate, infectious love for the Lord has always inspired me.

John carries a "love virus" that can only be caught in the secret place, where he learns to host God's presence. I have seen him live this message, even as he walked through the valley of the shadow of death. Through difficult seasons, I witnessed Jesus preparing a table for him in the presence of his enemies. In all circumstances, John found sustenance in God's presence, making it a daily practice that leads to wholeness and holiness. John, your guide on this journey, is raw, real, relational, relevant, radical, and a revivalist.

The daily bread John serves is rich with power, love, and wisdom. I challenge both you and myself to invest 15 minutes each day in encountering God—to know Him, experience Him, and meet Him face to face. May we experience His nearness, His heart, His nature, and His ways, allowing love to become the mark of our true maturity. After encountering Him, we then encounter who we are—our identity, potential, values, desires, gifts, and limitations. These all begin to reflect the image of the One we behold, and He is the One we are becoming and will release to the world.

May your heart be hungry and your mind open as John, like a master chef, prepares daily meals at the table of God's presence. The best of who you are will only be discovered in His presence. Jesus will be your host, inviting you to His table where the cup of life overflows. John will serve you the daily bread, freshly prepared by Jesus. Come and see, and come and taste.

Dr. Leif Hetland
    President of *Global Mission Awareness*
    Author of *The Love Awakening*

Introduction

The Presence started as a book idea about the power of thankfulness several years ago and has now turned into a 4-volume series as a 365-day devotional. I wrote The Presence as a daily blog/newsletter originally on my Substack platform after struggling with how to bring this book together. My heart and vision was to inspire people to live daily in the presence of God through thanksgiving, worship, and wonder.

Every time I tried to write on the power of thanksgiving, I would only come up with more ideas and I couldn't pull a book together. I was so inspired whenever I wrote on this subject, but I couldn't bring my thoughts on the topic together in a unified way until I realized one day that The Presence would really work so much better as a daily devotional filled with short thoughts to help people draw near to God.

My friend Jake once told me about a book writing idea where you could write each chapter as a blog and let people comment and interact with your work while you were writing. To be honest, I didn't like the idea for my own personal style when I heard him share that with me. But when I realized I had a daily devotional to write, the idea returned to me and motivated me to put it to work.

I talked things over with Grace and said I really want to write this book as a daily blog, but I need to know how you feel about it. And as my biggest encouragement, she cheered me on and said go for it.

When I first started writing, I wasn't sure if this would be 30, 60 or 90 days; or if I could make it a full 365. So, I started writing usually in the evening and scheduling each daily post at 4am the next morning. A few days I forgot to write and scrambled to catch up. Some days felt like heaven on earth, where I was bursting with wonder and excitement. Other days felt completely cold emotionally. It felt like a grind at times but by the time I reached 90 days I thought that I could maybe do the whole year.

By the grace of God and my wife, I made it the whole year, of course. As we started the publishing process, it became apparent that this book could end up being over 1,000 pages, so my editor approached me with the idea of doing a multi-part series. Hence, *The Presence Series* was born.

The 4-part volumes are titled: *The Lord of the Presence, The Power of the Presence, The Pursuit of the Presence* and *The Wonder of the Presence*.

The Lord of the Presence covers January through March. This first volume starts with an overview of the major themes of this whole book series. From there, the rest of volume one is devoted to God's character and nature through His names, His attributes and the nature of God the Father and God the Son.

The Power of the Presence covers April through June. This second volume continues on Jesus, the Son of God, the Holy Spirit and Paul's writings on the Presence of God.

The Pursuit of the Presence covers July through September. This third volume comes from the Psalms, the Prophets and the tabernacle of Moses.

The Wonder of the Presence covers October through December. This fourth and final volume begins with more on the tabernacles, the temples and the corporate presence of God throughout the Scriptures. It is wrapped up with a collection of thoughts on wonder and thanksgiving that lead up to the Incarnation throughout December. And finally, everything comes together as we focus on the return of Jesus, where all the saints will be with God forever in His manifest presence.

Each day begins with a Scripture reading and usually some kind of personal story or illustration from life. Then each daily devotional ends with a prayer. This work is Christ-centered, Trinitarian, simple and yet filled with theology. It's charismatic and promotes a Spirit-filled life of devotion.

I still don't feel qualified to share a work like this because I still need to grow in my own devotion in spending time alone in God's presence. Even in this season of publishing, I have been repenting of time wasters and distractions that I have let disrupt my time alone with Jesus. I offer this book not as an expert but as a fellow sojourner who is learning to frame success in life by being with Jesus and becoming more like Him.

I offer you this work with humility. Thank you for taking it up. May God use this work to grow your longing for the only One who can fulfill the longing of your soul, and may He be exalted in your life as you read and apply this work to your life.

Presence Mentors
October 1

The Lord said to Moses, "Come up to me on the mountain and stay here, and I will give you the tablets of stone with the law and commandments I have written for their instruction." Then Moses set out with Joshua his aide, and Moses went up on the mountain of God. He said to the elders, "Wait here for us until we come back to you. Aaron and Hur are with you, and anyone involved in a dispute can go to them." When Moses went up on the mountain, the cloud covered it, and the glory of the Lord settled on Mount Sinai. For six days the cloud covered the mountain, and on the seventh day the Lord called to Moses from within the cloud. To the Israelites the glory of the Lord looked like a consuming fire on top of the mountain. Then Moses entered the cloud as he went on up the mountain. And he stayed on the mountain forty days and forty nights.
Exodus 24:12-18

Have you ever been mentored in prayer or in practicing the Presence?

When I first got delivered and set free in my early twenties, I tried to get to church every time I could. I went to services, conferences and prayer meetings. I wanted to be in the Presence no matter what.

I learned a lot about encountering the Presence through men like my dad, Todd, and Bob at Man Prayer on Friday mornings. I also prayed with a man named Alan who was a little older than my dad on Monday nights.

Alan prayed in King James English with Thee and Thou type of addresses to the Lord. Our styles were different across our generations, but I learned how to lay hold of God with Alan. God's glory and Presence filled our sanctuary in such a holy way when we prayed together.

One of the best ways to grow in encountering the Presence is to go before the Lord with someone else who is further down the road than you.

Moses left behind the Israelites and even the elders to get the heavenly blueprints on the Tabernacle, as well as the 10 Commandments.

But he didn't leave behind Joshua.

Repeatedly, we see Moses is accompanied by Joshua. Moses saw the importance of equipping the next generation to behold the glory of God.

Joshua saw the importance of staying close and not missing out on the glory of God.

As a young man, I had to learn how to dwell before the Lord and not be impatient in prayer. I had to learn about the power of praise and thanksgiving.

I learned not to pray my own desires but to pray the Word of God.

I learned how to lead others in faith so that Jesus would show up in a manifest way among His people. I wouldn't know the Presence like I do if it hadn't been for those who have taught me how to pray.

There are several I could mention, and I owe them a debt of love and gratitude.

Don't pray alone all the time.

Find others, partners and mentors, to go in the glory along with you.

If you are further down the road, bring others who are new to prayer along and open up your heart before the Lord in such a way that He visits you with His glorious Presence.

Let us multiply lovers of Jesus by spending time at His feet and sitting with others while we do it.

———

Lord, I want to go before You and encounter Your glorious Presence more and more. Help me get alone in my secret place, but help me also to join others who are further ahead and those who need to go deeper. Mentor me through others and help me mentor others. Let the generations love Your glory like Moses and Joshua. In Jesus' name, amen.

Strange Fire
October 2

Aaron's sons Nadab and Abihu took their censers, put fire in them and added incense; and they offered unauthorized fire before the Lord, contrary to his command. So fire came out from the Presence of the Lord and consumed them, and they died before the Lord. Moses then said to Aaron, "This is what the Lord spoke of when he said: "'Among those who approach me I will be proved holy; in the sight of all the people I will be honored.'" Aaron remained silent.
Leviticus 10:1-3

Have you ever been around fire with someone you don't trust?
Growing up, we lived in what might seem like a pretty typical American middle-class suburb type of neighborhood. We played outside a lot growing up. We rode bikes, played basketball, baseball, hide and seek, and went on adventures in the woods.

We had some neighbor friends who we had a lot of fun with, but we also had some neighbors who got kind of wild. The neighbors that got wild had some pretty crazy parties, which were even broken up by the police.

At one of these parties during the Fourth of July, a neighbor got so drunk he launched large illegal fireworks down the street with a slingshot.

One of the other neighbors was standing nearby and got knocked off their feet by the explosion.

An altercation nearly happened.

What am I trying to say?

Fire in the hands of the wrong person is dangerous.

A lot of times, fire in the Bible was a holy and precious thing. The fire in the tabernacle on the altar and on the lampstand was a beautiful and holy thing. But God had a prescribed way that His people and His priests were supposed to approach Him.

Leviticus has many instructions about the sacrifices and the tabernacle. But in Leviticus 10, Aaron's sons brought strange or unauthorized fire before the Lord and a greater fire came from the Presence and killed them.

I love the Presence, but we must not become flippant or casual with God in how we approach Him.

In the New Testament awakening and outpouring in the book of Acts, Ananias and Sapphira were slain for lying to the Holy Spirit.

It's not common that people are killed in judgement by the Lord, but there is something about His holy Presence that increases the stakes of how we respond to the Lord.

People have different interpretations of what strange or unauthorized fire is before the Lord for our modern-day applications.

We can see the root cause of the sons of Aaron being slain was that the fire they offered was contrary to His command. They went before the Lord in direct disobedience to what He prescribed.

God calls us to be holy, and He has taught us we can only come to Him through the finished work of Jesus by the Holy Spirit.

May we fear the Lord and be obedient to Him so that we don't offer strange fire but only holy fire.

———

Lord Jesus, You are holy. Forgive me for any way that I have become causal or flippant in Your Presence. I repent for any areas of disobedience. Cleanse me. I want no part of strange or false fire. I want the true Presence of Your Spirit, and I want the holy flame of Your love. Purify me and ignite me with Your fire. In Your name, amen.

The Lost Ark
October 3

David conferred with each of his officers, the commanders of thousands and commanders of hundreds. He then said to the whole assembly of Israel, "If it seems good to you and if it is the will of the Lord our God, let us send word far and wide to the rest of our people throughout the territories of Israel, and also to the priests and Levites who are with them in their towns and pasturelands, to come and join us. Let us bring the ark of our God back to us, for we did not inquire of it during the reign of Saul." The whole assembly agreed to do this, because it seemed right to all the people.
1 Chronicles 13:1-4

Have you ever lost something so important that you felt deeply unsettled until you found it?

The day after our wedding day, Grace and I traveled to Kauai for our honeymoon.

Just a day or two into our trip, we went snorkeling. My mask had a crack in it, and I stood up in the shallow ocean to look at it. While looking at my mask, I noticed my wedding ring (that I had for just a few days now) was missing from my finger.

I told Grace, and we both started to panic.

I retraced my steps to the car.

She was frantically searching in the water with her mask.

We were praying in the Spirit.

She got really sad and started crying.

I was really sad too but grabbed her mask to keep looking through the rocks and shifting sands beneath us.

While I was looking, a woman who could tell we were looking for something approached Grace.

She asked her a few questions about what we were looking for and gave her my ring. Her boyfriend was a diver and found it on the ocean floor. What a sweet relief and joy to have back what was lost.

David realized during his reign that the Ark of the Covenant had not been central to Israelite worship under King Saul.

At one point, the Philistines stole the Ark and broke out in tumors, so they returned it.

But Saul and the people of Israel lost the importance of having the Ark and the Presence at their center. They did not minister to the Lord as He prescribed, and David said they did not inquire of it during Saul's reign.

If God's Presence has lost its prominence in Your life, would you do anything to search Him out again?

Is the Presence your priority?

Are you okay living without God's glory in your life?

Complacency about the Presence will cause us to lose the manifestation of His glory in our lives and churches.

We don't earn His nearness, but we have to stay thankful and prioritize being with Him. There are many distractions and good reasons that we often have for not letting His Presence be central in our lives.

But we should have a posture that we can't live without Him. We should stay hungry and desperate, so that if His Presence is not our priority, we would do anything to get Him back.

Be like King David and his honor and pursuit of the Ark of God's Presence.

Do whatever you need to do to recover God's Presence in your midst.

Lord Jesus, I love Your Presence. Let me stay hungry and desperate for Your Presence. Without You I have nothing. May I be diligent to pursue You and not let complacency enter into my life. I love the place Your glory dwells. You are my reward and prize. In Your name, amen.

The Cart and the Curse
October 4

They set the ark of God on a new cart and brought it from the house of Abinadab, which was on the hill. Uzzah and Ahio, sons of Abinadab, were guiding the new cart with the ark of God on it, and Ahio was walking in front of it. David and all Israel were celebrating with all their might before the Lord, with castanets, harps, lyres, timbrels, sistrums and cymbals. When they came to the threshing floor of Nakon, Uzzah reached out and took hold of the ark of God, because the oxen stumbled. The Lord's anger burned against Uzzah because of his irreverent act; therefore God struck him down, and he died there beside the ark of God. Then David was angry because the Lord's wrath had broken out against Uzzah, and to this day that place is called Perez Uzzah.
2 Samuel 6:3-8

Do you like taking shortcuts?
We live in a world that loves shortcuts, advantages and cheat codes.
When we were at a theme park recently, we could purchase additional passes to get us through the lines more quickly than others.

We already had to pay a handsome sum to get into the park, but for more money, we could save time and bypass the wait.

Our highways are now incorporating express toll lanes, where we can bypass traffic for a fee.

Where our world gets busier and busier, we value shortcuts over patience. We really don't want to be inconvenienced.

King David was honorable in his heart to desire the return of the Ark of the Covenant, the place of the Presence. But when he sought to bring the Ark back, they set the Ark on a cart. Everyone was so excited. They accompanied the Ark with celebration and praise with musical instruments.

But when the cart stumbled, Uzzah reached out to grab the Ark and God in His anger struck him dead. David was angry and had to pause bringing the Ark back.

We can only approach God on His terms.

In Exodus 25 and Numbers 4, the Lord instructed the priests to carry the Ark on the poles and cover it. But David and the Israelites pushed the Ark on a cart like the Philistines moved it.

It doesn't matter how sincere we are in our pursuit of the Lord if we are approaching Him in disobedience. Even if we worship with passion and praise, but we do it in the midst of disobedience, what should be a blessing to us becomes a curse. God cannot bless our disobedience.

I wonder how often I have used a cart in my worship and pursuit of the Presence?

I don't like being inconvenienced, and I don't enjoy wasting time.

Rushing and taking shortcuts, however, contradicts the very nature of hosting the Presence.

We don't earn our way into His Presence, but remember, the Presence is Him.

The Presence is His nearness, where we fellowship and relate to Him. It's the place our love is exchanged.

My wife does not appreciate me trying to take shortcuts in my time with her. If she gets the sense that she is more like a project to be checked off a list than my wife to be known and loved, she is rightfully alarmed.

God is worth the lavishing of our time and our careful obedience.

Patience and obedience are so good for us and bring glory to Him. Don't be in a hurry.

Rachel Hickson once shared a word God spoke to her, "Slow down, accomplish more." *

It's a paradox, but it's so true.

Our relationship with God's glorious Presence is about taking our time with Him in patient obedience.

Lord God, forgive me for being in a hurry and serving time more than serving You. You are worthy of my patient obedience. I come before You in humility and praise for the work of Your Son to give me access to Your glory. Help me slow down and yield to You. Deliver me from the deception of any carts I have relied upon to host Your Presence. In Jesus' name, amen

Presence Blessing
October 5

David was afraid of the Lord that day and said, "How can the ark of the Lord ever come to me?" He was not willing to take the ark of the Lord to be with him in the City of David. Instead, he took it to the house of Obed-Edom the Gittite. The ark of the Lord remained in the house of Obed-Edom the Gittite for three months, and the Lord blessed him and his entire household.
2 Samuel 6:9-11

Who is your favorite person to see?

I am returning home on a plane as I write this from almost a week away from my family.

I love seeing my wife. I love to be present with her because it brings me pleasure, and I know it pleases her to be near me.

It's the same for my children. Getting to reunite with family or an old friend is such a blessing.

The blessing is having them near.

David was in fear after Uzzah died and he had an ache, a longing in his soul to have the Ark back with him. He wasn't sure what to do yet, so he left the Ark at Obed-Edom's house for three months. When the Ark was with Obed-Edom, God blessed him and all of his house.

The blessing of the Presence is God Himself dwelling with us.

But it just so happens that in His Presence, all we need is there in Him. When He is close, His blessings are close.

My friend Raul Dimov recently shared that God's Presence is always connected to His pleasure. When God is present with us, He is pleased with us.

He is pleased to bless us as we host Him.

Obed-Edom, his family and all he had (See 1 Chronicles 13) were blessed for three months because of God's Presence.

If we seek blessing in our lives, we should first seek His Presence. We should desire to please the Lord and attract Him to dwell with us. God's favor rests on those that host His glory.

God is our reward and simply being with Him is our greatest delight.

But when we simply dwell with Him, He blesses our relationships and the work of our hands. May we all desire to host God's glorious Presence in our homes.

May our spouses, children, family and roommates come under the blessing of God because we prioritize hosting the Presence in our homes and lives.

―――――

Lord God, I love You and I love Your Presence. Teach me how to host Your Presence in my home and life. Let my home and my family delight in hosting You. Dwell with us and bless us. I seek You not for blessing first, but I'm thankful for all the ways You bless me when You are near. In Jesus' name, amen.

Undignified Reverence
October 6

David said to Michal, "It was before the Lord, who chose me rather than your father or anyone from his house when he appointed me ruler over the Lord's people Israel—I will celebrate before the Lord. I will become even more undignified than this, and I will be humiliated in my own eyes. But by these slave girls you spoke of, I will be held in honor."
2 Samuel 6:21-22

Do you like to dance?

One thing I love about children is how much they just naturally dance when music comes on.

When my children were growing up, we had so many dance parties.

Dance is a way to celebrate and enjoy life. Dance is even a way to worship the Lord. It seems that many Christians have become too dignified to dance and they are missing out on a chance to bring God reverence.

We might think that reverence and dance don't fit together in the same sentence or in the same action. But King David exemplifies both reverence and undignified dance when He finally leads the people in the return of the Ark from Obed-Edom's house to the City of David.

David realized how blessed Obed-Edom was and he longed to get the Ark back. They realized no one can touch the glory. There is a reverence required to come before the Presence.

This time, they carry the Ark instead of pushing it on a cart.

David is very intentional, and He makes a sacrifice as they carry the Ark.

The people join David in celebration, shouts, the blasting of trumpets and dance.

David dances in His linen ephod which is his undergarments.

This deeply offends his wife Michal, who is the daughter of Saul. She is angry at her husband and David replies, "It was before the Lord... I will become ever more undignified."

David had a deep reverence for the Presence, so much so that he wanted to show His full commitment and love to the Lord publicly, even if he looked foolish. David may have looked a little crazy, but he didn't seem to care because he is crazy for His God. David was wholehearted and instead of being casual before the Lord, was fully committed to honoring Him with every step.

David was not a perfect man. He had many faults and failures, but He loved God and His manifest Presence maybe more than anyone in Scripture (besides Jesus Himself).

When we reverence God, we should be willing to look the fool in our love for Him. God is worthy to be worshiped and praised with great celebration and humility. God's Presence and glory should set us to dancing.

Like David, are you willing to become more undignified in your praise?

May we not care about what others think, but may we take every step in His Presence with His glory and pleasure in mind.

Almighty God, You are worthy of my reverence and my celebration. I dance before You. I will become more undignified. You are worthy of a sold-out heart that does not care what others think about my praise. Let me be intentional in my praise and bring You pleasure. In Jesus' name, amen.

David's Tabernacle
October 7

After David had constructed buildings for himself in the City of David, he prepared a place for the ark of God and pitched a tent for it. Then David said, "No one but the Levites may carry the ark of God, because the Lord chose them to carry the ark of the Lord and to minister before him forever."
1 Chronicles 15:1-2

If you are a parent, have you ever had a child do something unexpected that really blessed your heart?

When my kids have gone out of the way to bless my heart or my wife's, there is nothing quite like it.

When a child prepares a special meal, writes a card or cleans up without being asked, the level of delight in my heart as a parent is hard to match.

You do so much for your children as a parent that when they, of their own volition, think of doing something for you that you haven't asked them to, it's a great honor.

The story of David's Tabernacle or David's Tent is interesting.

When David attempted to move the Ark to the City of David and Uzzah was struck dead, He realized he needed to do things God's way.

David reinstated the Levites to carry the Ark as God has prescribed. He wouldn't do it wrong.

But instead of keeping the Ark in the Tabernacle of Moses at Shiloh, David kept the Ark out in the open under His own tabernacle.

We see nothing in the Scriptures that says God told David to make this major switch of ministering to the Ark in his tent instead of the Tabernacle of Moses.

So, where David wouldn't violate how to carry the Ark any longer, He did invent a new way to minister before the Ark, which was motivated by His love for the Presence of the Lord.

David's Tabernacle, as seen in the rest of 1 Chronicles, was a place that Levites, musicians and singers ministered to the Lord around the clock by bringing sacrifices to the Lord and praising Him with songs.

Many of the Psalms would have been sung by the worshippers at the tabernacle. David literally hosted the Presence of the Lord by ministering to Him at the Ark of the Covenant.

This pleased the Lord and His favor rested upon David and Israel through this 24-7 worship and praise.

The Lord is worthy to be worshiped by His people.

There is never a moment in life when He is not worthy of worship.

Be extravagant in Your praise.

Your home and your church can become a place where you host God's Presence through worship as you minister to the Lord. Your worship and praise touch the heart of the Lord.

Come before Him in song and in dance.

Write Him your own song.

Write Him a letter of love.

Do something like David to move the heart of God and bring Him praise.

Set aside time to bring the Lord uncommon praise.

Lord, You are worthy of my worship. You are worthy of worship and praise around the clock. Every minute of every day, You are worthy to be praised. Teach me how to minister to You and host Your Presence. Teach Your church how to minister unto You and host Your Presence. Give us songs and sounds that will touch Your heart and bring You glory. In Jesus' name, amen.

The Tent Restored
October 8

When they finished, James spoke up. "Brothers," he said, "listen to me. Simon has described to us how God first intervened to choose a people for his name from the Gentiles. The words of the prophets are in agreement with this, as it is written: "'After this I will return and rebuild David's fallen tent. Its ruins I will rebuild, and I will restore it, that the rest of mankind may seek the Lord, even all the Gentiles who bear my name, says the Lord, who does these things'— things known from long ago.
Acts 15:13-18

Have you ever experienced the restoration of something long lost?

I can't say I've had something that was long lost restored. But I can imagine that if it's something of great financial or emotional value, it would be a tremendous experience.

My wife and I watched a film recently about a Jewish woman who was an Austrian citizen. Her family had a piece of art stolen by the Nazis and decades later, after a lengthy series of legal battles, she had the art restored to her.

God longed for the restoration of something.

He longed for the restoration of David's Tent.

The Tabernacle of David was a prototype of New Covenant worship and outreach for the Gentiles (those who are non-Jews). In the book of Acts, as the gospel is spreading to the Gentiles, the apostles quote the prophet Amos, who is speaking for the Lord, saying that He will rebuild and restore David's tabernacle.

Different scholars believe different things about what this might look like, but we can see that God loved the worship David and Israel brought from the heart in this Tent.

David was a forerunner who modeled that worship would not be centered on ritual and performance, but on praise that comes from the heart.

Part of God's plan for the gospel to go forth to all nations is for praise to go up in the earth as David led Israel to do.

God is accepting worship from all nations.

He is still looking for worship that is in reverence and is according to what He prescribes, but there is also great freedom in how we come before Him.

David's Tent shows us that God is worthy to be worshipped 24-7.

David's Tent shows us that God loves to be worshipped with singing, instruments, and dancing.

David's Tent shows us that God longs to be worshipped by all nations and cultures.

David's Tent shows us that God delights in worship that is passionate and from the heart.

Davids Tent shows us that worship from the heart means we can boldly approach and encounter the Presence.

Lord God, thank You for showing me the type of worship that You love. I get to move Your heart as I participate in the restoration of David's tabernacle. Let me bring You worship and praise that is wholehearted in my love for You. In Jesus' name, amen.

DAVID'S DREAM
OCTOBER 9

After the king was settled in his palace and the Lord had given him rest from all his enemies around him, he said to Nathan the prophet, "Here I am, living in a house of cedar, while the ark of God remains in a tent." Nathan replied to the king, "Whatever you have in mind, go ahead and do it, for the Lord is with you."
2 Samuel 7:1-3

Have you ever had a dream of doing something great?

I had many dreams growing up of doing great things.

I dreamed of being a firefighter and saving people's lives.

I dreamed of being an inventor and solving problems people didn't know they had, all the while making lots of money off my inventions.

I dreamed of making the game-winning shot at the buzzer or game-winning hit in the last inning.

I think we have all dreamed of doing something great in our lives.

King David had a dream in His heart to build a temple, a house for the Lord.

It's difficult to tell if David actually realized that his dream was a part of God's eternal plan for Jerusalem. David wanted to build a temple in what was called the City of David and what would be called Jerusalem hundreds of years later.

This Tent where the Ark of the Covenant rested was also known as the place of Zion. Many of David's Psalms refer to Zion or Mount Zion. This is the place that David and those in his Tabernacle encountered the Presence as they ministered to the Lord around the clock.

This place of worship and of the dwelling place of God would become the city of the Great King. This city Jerusalem, with the Temple built there, would become the place where Jesus suffered and died on the cross, was buried and rose again, and where He will return one day when He comes back to establish His kingdom.

David was called by the Lord, a man after My own heart (See Acts 13:22).

The Lord forbids David from building the Temple because of all the blood that David shed in war, but He allowed him to prepare for it so his son Solomon could build it.

But even in all of David's failures and bloodshed, the Lord still saw David as a man after His own heart.

David partnered with the dream of God for His Presence and saw in his times alone with the Lord the coming Messiah. So much came out of David's time in the Presence of the Lord that Jesus is even called the Son of David.

Our times in the Presence are all owed to David's obedience and partnership with the heart of God. There is no telling what vision may arise in our heart as we fellowship with the Son of David.

We can host God's Presence as David did through continual praise and worship. Time alone with our King awakens in us the dream that God has for our lives that just might benefit others as well.

Lord Jesus, Son of David, You are the King of kings and Lord of lords. I worship You. Let me dream the dreams that come from partnership with Your heart. I want to dwell with You now, while I wait for Your return to the great city of Jerusalem one day. You are worthy of my worship and my obedience. In Jesus' name, amen.

Solomon's Temple
October 10

Then King Solomon summoned into his Presence at Jerusalem the elders of Israel, all the heads of the tribes and the chiefs of the Israelite families, to bring up the ark of the Lord's covenant from Zion, the City of David... The priests then brought the ark of the Lord's covenant to its place in the inner sanctuary of the temple, the Most Holy Place, and put it beneath the wings of the cherubim... When the priests withdrew from the Holy Place, the cloud filled the temple of the Lord. And the priests could not perform their service because of the cloud, for the glory of the Lord filled his temple. Then Solomon said, "The Lord has said that he would dwell in a dark cloud; I have indeed built a magnificent temple for you, a place for you to dwell forever."
1 Kings 8:1, 6, 10-13

Have you ever experienced a cloud of God's glory?

Have you ever been in a place of worship where you couldn't really stand up or couldn't keep doing what you were doing?

I've never been in a physical cloud of glory, but I've had some pretty incredible moments in the Presence of God where I felt God all around me in a supernatural way.

God's glorious Presence comes upon us as a sign of His pleasure.

Solomon was able to build and complete the Temple that his father David had envisioned and prepared him to build. In 1 Kings 8, when the Ark of the Covenant was brought into the new Temple for dedication, there was a cloud of God's glory that filled the temple. This cloud was so thick and powerful that the priests could not continue to perform their duties.

Those who know the Presence long for these times in God's glory where we can't stand up, move, or continue in our normal course of action.

Pastor Bill Johnson often told a story about Smith Wigglesworth praying with other pastors and leaders. A man heard that God's glory would come so strong that people couldn't stay in the room and would have to leave while Smith prayed. This man resolved in his heart that he would not leave the prayer meeting, but even with his resolve, he too had to leave the room along with all others because of the intensity of God's Presence. *

Solomon's Temple being dedicated was blessed by the Presence.

Solomon had the opportunity to live out a generational blessing of being a man of God's Presence like his dad did.

There is no greater legacy that we could receive or pass on in our generations then to be a person of the Presence. There is weighty intense glory available for us when we make our lives, homes and churches a place that God desires to dwell.

Lord God, I love Your Presence. There is no one like You. Help me make my life, my home and my church a place that You desire to dwell. I want to encounter Your Presence in real and tangible ways that stops me in my tracks. I want to experience Your glory and pass on this love to the next generation. In Jesus' name, amen.

Revival and Reformation Presence

October 11

After the wall had been rebuilt and I had set the doors in place, the gatekeepers, the musicians and the Levites were appointed.
Nehemiah 7:1

What is the greatest thing you have ever built?

I don't know what the greatest thing I've ever built is for sure, because I haven't done much building.

I've picked up a few very basic abilities from watching my father-in-law and brother-in-law help me on various houses we have owned do repairs. They are both skilled carpenters.

But what makes something great that you build?

Is it not the purpose for which you are building it?

Israel and Judah experienced the judgment of God because of their idolatry and unfaithfulness to the covenant that God made with them. But God promised great restoration to His people after seventy years of judgment.

Ezra and Nehemiah are the books in the Bible that contain the history of the great revival and reformation that took place through the leadership of these two men of God.

Ezra led the people as a priest and restored the importance of the Scriptures in the life of Israel. Nehemiah led the people in construction and the rebuilding of the wall. They both had to endure great opposition to rebuild the city of Jerusalem.

The rebuilding of the wall in Jerusalem and the Temple were ultimately to bring the purpose of the city and the Temple back to its original intent that David had for the Tabernacle.

The people repented, obeyed the Scripture and returned to prayer.

Nehemiah helped see the appointing of gatekeepers, musicians and Levites so the Presence could be restored.

This is the purpose of revival and restoration, to restore the preeminence of God's Presence in our lives through true worship.

When our homes, churches, cities and nations fall short of God's intended design for us, we need to return to the ways that God instituted.

Returning to God's ways of faithfulness to His covenant and to worship brings about reformation and revival.

When we rebuild what is broken, God will come and dwell with us again.

God is merciful and good! He loves to return to us when we return to Him!

When the Presence seems lost, God is always raising up a remnant to rebuild for revival and reformation. There is no greater cause than the cause of Christ in each generation. When you sense that things are lost, it could be that God is sharing His heart with you to be a part of the revival and reformation process.

Lord, I want to be a part of a revival and reformation in my church and in my city. Have Your way in me and use me to pray and lead in a way that rebuilds families, homes and cities. Make my life, my home, my church and my city a dwelling place for Your Presence. In Jesus' name, amen.

From the Temple to the Christ
October 12

When it was almost time for the Jewish Passover, Jesus went up to Jerusalem. In the temple courts he found people selling cattle, sheep and doves, and others sitting at tables exchanging money. So he made a whip out of cords, and drove all from the temple courts, both sheep and cattle; he scattered the coins of the money changers and overturned their tables. To those who sold doves he said, "Get these out of here! Stop turning my Father's house into a market!" His disciples remembered that it is written: "Zeal for your house will consume me." The Jews then responded to him, "What sign can you show us to prove your authority to do all this?" Jesus answered them, "Destroy this temple, and I will raise it again in three days." They replied, "It has taken forty-six years to build this temple, and you are going to raise it in three days?" But the temple he had spoken of was his body. After he was raised from the dead, his disciples recalled what he had said. Then they believed the scripture and the words that Jesus had spoken.
John 2:13-22

Have you ever had a friend who spoke in mysteries or riddles?

I was never the best at solving riddles.

Some people love mysterious language and riddles that are perplexing to solve.

Jesus used mysterious language many times in parables and other challenging statements. He frequently did this to stir a deeper longing in those eager to understand Him.

In John 2, Jesus cleanses the Temple and does not like to see the corruption and greed in His Father's house.

But then this mysterious statement from Jesus comes forth, that if the Temple is destroyed, He will rebuild it in three days.

John immediately interprets this to mean Jesus was speaking of His body.

The disciples eventually understood this after Jesus was crucified, buried, and raised from the dead.

This is a little review if you have been following along all year with me in this series. However, it's crucial to remember God's Presence with His people—first in Moses' Tabernacle, then David's, and finally Solomon's Temple—all foreshadowing His dwelling with us through Jesus.

Jesus' body became the new Temple.

God fulfilled the meaning of the Temple in the person and body of His Son, Jesus. Jesus is how we would now enter the Presence.

Jesus still cares about the state of His Father's house, the church. He will confront us and cleanse us when we have gotten off course in making Him our central focus as His people gather.

Jesus is passionate that our worship and ministry is pure and that the church is a place where all people have an authentic encounter with God.

———

Lord Jesus, thank You for the beautiful fulfillment and completeness of You being the Temple for us. You are the place where heaven meets earth, and the Presence of God has been opened up for me. Let my worship be pure and acceptable to You. I love Your passion for Your Father's House. In Jesus' name, amen.

From Moses to Jesus to Us
October 13

Therefore, holy brothers and sisters, who share in the heavenly calling, fix your thoughts on Jesus, whom we acknowledge as our apostle and high priest. He was faithful to the one who appointed him, just as Moses was faithful in all God's house. Jesus has been found worthy of greater honor than Moses, just as the builder of a house has greater honor than the house itself. For every house is built by someone, but God is the builder of everything. "Moses was faithful as a servant in all God's house," bearing witness to what would be spoken by God in the future. But Christ is faithful as the Son over God's house. And we are his house, if indeed we hold firmly to our confidence and the hope in which we glory.
Hebrews 3:1-6

What makes a special house so special?

Well, a special house might be special because of the design, architecture or decor.

But I think the most special homes I have ever visited are because of the hosts.

The way the host treats me and my family makes the difference in what separates a special house from all the others. The host creates the atmosphere, the attitude, the decor, the feel and the order of the house.

The host is what makes a house a home.

Moses was the head of God's house, the Tabernacle, but Jesus became the faithful Son over God's house, the church.

The writer of Hebrews is talking about the greatness of Moses overseeing the Tabernacle and the people of Israel, but now One greater than Moses oversees the house of the Lord.

And we are that house.

The church has become the New Tabernacle, the dwelling place of God's glory and the host of the Presence.

Our buildings are not the house of God, we the people are the house of God.

If Moses built God's house in the Old Testament and had such an incredible manifestation of God's glory, ought not God's house in the New Testament have a greater manifestation of glory since it was built by Jesus?

Jesus is the faithful Overseer, Builder, Apostle and High Priest of His house. He is greater than the house He has built.

What a privilege it is for us to be the people of His house.

There is no one like the Lord Jesus.

He is our God, and we are His people.

He is the Head and the Host of His house.

He became the Temple or the House of God, but He built us into this house as the Head of the body who have put our "confidence and hope in which we glory" in Him.

We are now together as God's people, the House in which He dwells.

Lord Jesus, thank You for redeeming me and giving me confidence and hope in You. You have built Your church to be Your House. Thank you for bringing me into the church, which is Your body, and making me a part of this glorious place where You dwell. You deserve all the honor and glory. In Your holy name, amen.

Corporate Presence
October 14

Don't you know that you yourselves are God's temple and that God's Spirit dwells in your midst? If anyone destroys God's temple, God will destroy that person; for God's temple is sacred, and you together are that temple.
1 Corinthians 3:16-17

What is something you can't do alone, but you need the help of others to accomplish?

American and Western culture tends to be individualistic.

There is nothing inherently wrong with the focus on individual responsibility or even individual faith in God. But we certainly can become wrong if that is the only way we see life.

We need others for many things in life.

Even if we can accomplish certain things on our own, it is usually because someone taught us, empowered us, or helped us in some way.

I am writing this devotional daily, but I can't do it without the

Lord's help, my wife's support, the Bible education I have received or the people that designed software, tablets and computers.

We need to realize we can't do much alone without community, but together with others, we can accomplish a lot.

Earlier in this series, I talked about how the individual believer becomes the temple of the Lord as one puts their faith in Christ and receives the Holy Spirit.

Which is absolutely true.

The Apostle Paul teaches this in 1 Corinthians 6, but what is often missed is He also teaches that we together are the temple of the Holy Spirit as the church. You see, there is a corporate Presence we experience as the temple of the Holy Spirit in the church when we are together that we cannot experience alone.

This is exactly what Paul is saying in 1 Corinthians 3, that the church at Corinth, even with her flaws and failures, is the very temple of God and His Spirit dwells in their midst.

He has such strong words that if anyone tries to destroy the church, God's new temple (the people of the New Covenant), He will destroy them because the temple is sacred.

Did you catch that?

The church is the temple that is sacred.

We together are the sacred temple of God, the dwelling of the Holy Spirit.

We can't fully experience the Presence of God on our own. We undeniably experience God's presence in our personal relationship with Him, as the Holy Spirit dwells within us. But there is a great sense of the Presence we can only encounter together as God's sacred temple.

This is the corporate Presence.

This is what it means to be the church.

I am not the church, and I am not the whole temple. But I am a part of the church and together we are the temple of the Holy Spirit.

Lord God, thank You for letting me be a part of Your temple, the church. Help me love the church and treat her as sacred. Let my church where I belong live in the truth that we are a sacred dwelling place for Your Holy Spirit to be in our midst. Let us experience Your corporate Presence as we gather. In Jesus' name, amen.

The Dwelling Plan A
October 15

Consequently, you are no longer foreigners and strangers, but fellow citizens with God's people and also members of his household, built on the foundation of the apostles and prophets, with Christ Jesus himself as the chief cornerstone. In him the whole building is joined together and rises to become a holy temple in the Lord. And in him you too are being built together to become a dwelling in which God lives by his Spirit.

...and to make plain to everyone the administration of this mystery, which for ages past was kept hidden in God, who created all things. His intent was that now, through the church, the manifold wisdom of God should be made known to the rulers and authorities in the heavenly realms, according to his eternal purpose that he accomplished in Christ Jesus our Lord.
Ephesians 2:19-22, 3:9-11

Are you a person who likes to have a Plan B?

Or do you only like to have a Plan A?

To me, it can feel like having a Plan B is conceding defeat by preparing for plan A not to work out. Of course, this shouldn't always be the case. It is okay and even beneficial to plan for certain things in life, with multiple variables for outcomes.

But I just admire someone who goes all in on a plan and sticks to it without expecting failure or other options than mission success.

The church is God's Plan A as a dwelling place, a temple for His glory, the Presence.

Paul is saying exactly this in Ephesians 2 and 3. The church is built on Jesus, the apostles and prophets.

Another way we could say it is that the church is built on the person and work of Christ and the Scriptures (the Word of God through the apostles and prophets that reveal Christ).

This is the dwelling place we are when we come together, where God lives by His Spirit.

Paul continues to unfold that we, the church, are the eternal plan of God that was hidden in times past but has now been revealed. God always planned to have a church made up of Jew and Gentile, together being a holy temple where He dwells in the earth.

When God dwelled in Eden, in Moses' Tabernacle, David's sacred Tent and Solomon's temple, He always had us, the church in mind.

The church is so mysterious and powerful that we are revealing God's plan of wisdom to rulers and powers in the heavens. The church caught the spirit world by surprise.

When we gather in our cities to sing and worship, we are not simply doing a religious duty, we are gathering as a supernatural dwelling for God's glory that serves notice to dark rulers in the spirit realm that Jesus is the victorious King!

May we never sell ourselves short or look at the church as an optional club to join or not.

We are the dwelling place for God according to His eternal plan.

We are God's plan A!

Father God, what a marvelous plan to build the church of Jew and Gentile as a dwelling for Your glory and a bride for Your Son. Let me honor the church and contribute to the unfolding of Your eternal plan that is built on Christ and the apostles and prophets. Inhabit us, Your church, with Your glory. In Jesus' name, amen.

Living Stones
October 16

As you come to him, the living Stone—rejected by humans but chosen by God and precious to him— you also, like living stones, are being built into a spiritual house to be a holy priesthood, offering spiritual sacrifices acceptable to God through Jesus Christ. For in Scripture it says: "See, I lay a stone in Zion, a chosen and precious cornerstone, and the one who trusts in him will never be put to shame." Now to you who believe, this stone is precious. But to those who do not believe, "The stone the builders rejected has become the cornerstone," and, "A stone that causes people to stumble and a rock that makes them fall." They stumble because they disobey the message—which is also what they were destined for. But you are a chosen people, a royal priesthood, a holy nation, God's special possession, that you may declare the praises of him who called you out of darkness into his wonderful light. Once you were not a people, but now you are the people of God; once you had not received mercy, but now you have received mercy.

1 Peter 2:4-10

Have you ever seen a wall or building that is built of stones?

I love beautiful stonework. Whether it's an ancient castle or a modern wall, it is always amazing to me how a stone layer or mason fits all the stones together to make something that is strong and beautiful.

There is a certain skill involved in getting these small and broken pieces of stone to fit together and become something that none of these single pieces is without the others.

The church is God's temple.

The church is built on the Living Stone of Jesus Christ as the chosen and precious Cornerstone. Through faith in Jesus, we become like living stones, and we are built into a spiritual house as a holy priesthood.

Our ministry as priests is to bring spiritual sacrifices to God through Jesus Christ.

God assembles us all as living stones to come together as the church so that we might be priests unto God.

Our gathering as the church is as living stones who literally minister as priests to God in the Presence.

We don't come to church primarily for duty, to hear sermons, to sing songs, have social events or to pay tithes. We come together with the church to minister to the heart of God as priests.

This is who we are.

We are a priesthood of chosen people who are a royal and holy nation. We are God's special possession who declare God's praises, because He brought us out of darkness and into the light of His glorious Presence.

We must not replace our personal time with Jesus with church gatherings of corporate worship. But we must also not forsake the gathering together as living stones who minister together as a spiritual house. There is a glory of the Presence on our personal prayer lives and devotion to the Lord, but there is another sense of God's glory that we only experience as living stones when we are fitted together with one another.

Lord Jesus, our Living Cornerstone, let me and my church see our primary calling as priests who minister unto Your heart as a spiritual house. We were not a people, but You have made us Your people, for You called us out of darkness and into Your glorious light! Fit me together with Your holy people, the living stones, that we may be a dwelling place for Your Presence. In Your holy name, amen.

Teach Through Singing
October 17

Let the message of Christ dwell among you richly as you teach and admonish one another with all wisdom through psalms, hymns, and songs from the Spirit, singing to God with gratitude in your hearts.
Colossians 3:16

Have you ever heard people say that we aren't singing to one another but to God when we worship?

There are some funny church parody videos online with people singing about how great they are instead of how great God is.

Worship music isn't usually that self-focused but sometimes worship can become more about us than Him, which is problematic at best and grieving to God at worst.

We often judge the quality of worship based on our enjoyment of the music and the sound quality.

When we come together as the church, we are not singing to each other in the sense that we worship each other. Again, we come primarily as priests to minister to the Lord.

But part of our formation in the faith is to teach and admonish one another in our singing. I want to be very clear that worship should never lose the primary purpose of exalting God and ministering to His heart.

But in this place of worship, we are instructed to instruct one another through our singing to God.

When we come together to sing to God in psalms, hymns, and songs from the Spirit, we are teaching each other in the Presence. There is a part of our spiritual formation and discipleship that is shaped by the Presence in our singing that is not developed any other way.

Of course we are to sing alone, but something happens when the company of the saints comes together and sings rich Biblical truths about Jesus Christ.

It's one thing to mentally know and understand specific truths about the Scripture, but it's another thing to live in awe and wonder at these truths and apply them to your life in obedience.

The corporate church is important for us to worship together as we minister to God, but also for us to be shaped by what we sing.

Of course, it's important that our songs are rooted in sound doctrine and in the Scriptures, because what we sing will shape our spiritual affections.

As we allow the message of Christ to dwell in us richly, and the message of Christ dwells richly in our songwriters, we get to have a powerful encounter with the living Jesus in our midst and have our minds renewed in His truth.

Corporate encounters in worship are so important because they leave an imprint on our spiritual lives. The Lord loves the variety of psalms, hymns, and songs from the Spirit.

We should sing old songs and new songs that are full of the truth and beauty of Jesus.

―――

Lord Jesus, today I sing to You. Let the message of Christ dwell in me richly and let me not forsake coming together with the church corporately to sing psalms, hymns and spiritual songs. You are worthy Jesus! I love You and worship You! You fill my heart with gratitude for all You are! In Your name, amen.

Where it All Began
October 18

Now the Lord God had planted a garden in the east, in Eden; and there he put the man he had formed. The Lord God made all kinds of trees grow out of the ground—trees that were pleasing to the eye and good for food. In the middle of the garden were the tree of life and the tree of the knowledge of good and evil.
Genesis 2:8-9

Where is your favorite place to get some peace and quiet? Do you prefer something out in nature, a lake, river or the ocean? Do you like to get some peace and quiet in the woods?

Or do you like to be inside and maybe put on some music?

I like to be by the ocean or a river, but I can also really enjoy being at home if I have some of my favorite soothing music on.

God had a favorite place to visit with humankind, and it was the garden of Eden.

When God made the whole world, He placed Adam and Eve in the garden of Eden. Eden was God's favorite place; it was the place where He communed with His creation that He loved.

Eden is also known as Paradise, but I covered that before.

I want us to see that Eden was also the first type of tabernacle.

Before there was a tabernacle of Moses, David's sacred tent, Solomon's temple or even the church of Jesus Christ, there was Eden.

This garden was a sacred place where God came to visit Adam and Eve. After they sinned, God was coming to walk in the garden in the cool of the day to fellowship with them. He even asked them where they were.

We see this is the place where God dwells with humans. This is the place where heaven meets earth. This is the place of the Presence. These are all characteristics of a tabernacle or temple.

We learn at Eden that God being with Adam and Eve, means that a marriage and a family are sacred to God.

The Presence can dwell not only in a physical temple, but in the holy place of covenant human relationships. Our homes and families can host God's Presence.

Eden shows us God's passionate desire for Him to be with us.

God longs to walk with us not only individually, but corporately in the community of our homes, our marriages, our families, and our churches.

Eden is the first picture and experience of God's tabernacle with humankind.

May we invite God to walk with us in every rhythm of our lives in our homes, our yards, our workplace and our world.

Lord God, I know Your desire is to dwell with me and walk with me. Let my marriage, my home and my family be a tabernacle where You dwell in Your glory. I want to walk with You and let Your Presence permeate everything in my life. You are my God. I love to be with You. In Jesus' name, amen.

Registered in Heaven
October 19

But you have come to Mount Zion and to the city of the living God, the heavenly Jerusalem, to an innumerable company of angels, to the general assembly and church of the firstborn who are registered in heaven, to God the Judge of all, to the spirits of just men made perfect, to Jesus the Mediator of the new covenant, and to the blood of sprinkling that speaks better things than that of Abel. See that you do not refuse Him who speaks.
Hebrews 12:22-24

Have you registered for gifts for a wedding or a baby?

I remember how much fun I had registering for gifts with my wife before we were married. Time was moving so fast during that period of our life.

We were engaged for about four and a half months. We had to figure out where we were going to live, do our pre-marriage counseling, wedding planning and the gift registry.

Registering for gifts made the idea that we were building a life and a home together more real. Registering meant there was a future anticipation of receiving the things we needed for our new life together.

We who have faith in Christ are a part of the most glorious organization on the planet. The author of Hebrews describes us as "the general assembly and church of the firstborn who are registered in heaven."

Do you hear that?

We are registered in heaven.

The church of Jesus Christ is a heavenly organization.

It's like we have one foot on earth and one in heaven.

We've been registered.

We have the Presence now, but there is a greater Presence for us in the future.

Hebrews builds on this whole idea that Jesus is the fulfillment of the priesthood, the temple and tabernacle, and the sacrifice. The glory of God's Presence on all these Old Testament types has been fulfilled in Jesus and made even better for us.

Through Jesus, we now corporately as the church have come to Mount Zion, the heavenly Jerusalem, and we are surrounded by an innumerable company of angels. Angels are connected to the Presence. The church gathered together is a supernatural community.

We are a supernatural community because of the blood of Jesus.

We are connected to those who have gone before us.

The church has become the place where heaven meets earth.

The church is the place where the future glory of heaven is already breaking into our world now.

What a glorious inheritance we have in Christ and what an amazing company we belong to in the church.

Lord Jesus, thank You for purchasing me and cleansing me with Your blood. You are the Mediator of the new covenant, and You have brought me into Your church. What a glorious church it is. Let me live in the truth and depth of Your revelation of the church, the place like Mt. Zion, where Your glorious Presence dwells. In Your name Jesus, amen.

The Bride
October 20

Husbands, love your wives, just as Christ loved the church and gave himself up for her to make her holy, cleansing her by the washing with water through the word, and to present her to himself as a radiant church, without stain or wrinkle or any other blemish, but holy and blameless... This is a profound mystery—but I am talking about Christ and the church.
Ephesians 5:25-27, 32

If you are married, how do you show love to your spouse?

I love my wife, and I love showing that love to her by speaking life over her.

I am not a perfect husband, and I am on the long journey of learning from Jesus on how to love my bride. But one thing I do is make up corny songs about my wife. I compliment her every day and I speak the truth of God's Word over her. I love to wash her life with my words and, ultimately, the Word of God.

Paul teaches in Ephesians about how husbands and wives are to love and honor one another.

But in the midst of this teaching, Paul talks about Christ and the church. He says this is a profound mystery that Christian marriage, where a husband loves His wife like Christ loves the church and a wife submits to her husband, is a picture of Jesus and the church.

The church is the bride of Jesus.

I am not the bride of Jesus by myself, but the church corporately, we are the bride of Christ together. Together we experience the Presence of Jesus as a bride that is in love with her bridegroom.

One of the reasons we gather together is because Jesus loves us being together as His bride. He washes us as His bride with His Word so that we will one day be presented to Him as a radiant church, without stain or wrinkle, but holy and blameless.

This is the exchange of love we have together with the Lord as His people.

There is a way we receive the Word together that washes us, that we don't experience alone.

There is a way we love Jesus together that we don't love Him alone.

This is the love that Jesus has for us the church corporately as His bride and the love that we have for Him collectively.

Many get hurt and give up on the church, but Jesus loves the church and never gives up on her.

The church has flaws and failures, but Jesus is washing us and perfecting us for the future as the bride of Christ.

We are looking forward to that day.

We exist as the church now, but we are the bride forever.

If we are not a part of the church now, how can we be part of the bride forever?

May we love what and who Jesus loves, His bride, the church.

May we enter into the promise of being radiant, washed in His Word and ready for our future wedding day together.

———

Lord Jesus, thank You for Your love for me to put me in the church. Heal me of hurts from the church and let me love her as Your bride. Wash me and my church with the water of Your Word. Prepare us for Your Presence. Let us bring our love to You and receive Your love together as we are Your church. I love You! In Your name, amen.

God is Present
October 21

But there they are, overwhelmed with dread, for God is present in the company of the righteous.
Psalms 14:5

What are your friends like?

A man named Dan Pena is credited with the phrase, "Show me your friends and I'll show you your future."

There is a lot of truth to this statement.

I've heard others share wisdom that we become like the five people we spend the most time with.

Our friends have a major influence on us.

Our friends not only have a major influence on us in practical things, but they also have an influence on whether we experience more of the Presence.

David said that God is present in the company of the righteous.

The corporate Presence of God comes upon us in a way together that we don't experience alone (and yes, His Presence comes upon us alone in a way we don't experience with others around).

One day, I was at a conference my friend Ben Dixon was hosting, and he brought Todd White to minister.

That morning, we joined Todd in a small room for prayer. It was just the three of us. God was present in our company.

It was hard to describe, but we fell on our faces and could not get up. The weight of God's glory was upon us. We were marked in His Presence as we wept before Him, and a holy fear was stirred up in my life.

Each week we have been having prayer meetings where we minister to the Lord at our church. We have anywhere between 5 and 40 people that usually come to our times of prayer.

But God keeps coming.

A pastor friend dropped into one of these prayer meetings with about 5 of us and one worship leader on guitar. Heaven was opened and God was in our company.

He asked, "Is it always like this?"

Lately it has been more like that than not.

When we, the righteous, come together to seek Him, He is with us.

He is in our company.

Join with righteous friends who love Jesus in faith and get ready for an encounter with and in Him.

Your company will impact your encounter with the Presence

Lord Jesus, thank You for the church! Thank You for the company of the righteous! You are present in our company. Lord, I honor the gathering and coming together of Your saints. Manifest among us, Your people. Your Presence is our reward. In Your name, amen.

ENTHRONED
OCTOBER 22

> But You are holy, Enthroned in the praises of Israel.
> Psalms 22:3 NKJV

Have you ever seen a king or ruler on a throne?

The throne is a seat of authority in a kingdom, which is reserved for the king, queen, or other rulers.

Everyone else is on their feet.

The enthroned one gets to sit while others work and serve who is seated.

The rest of the kingdom honors and serves the ruler, who is enthroned.

The Messianic Psalm 22 is full of prophetic imagery that points to the suffering of Jesus. Near the beginning of this Psalm, we see that our suffering Messiah is also the King who sits enthroned upon the praises of Israel.

Praise creates a throne for God.

This is a community transforming truth, that our corporate praise builds a throne for God. The Presence manifests and rests upon the people of God who bring Him praise.

A company of people can host God. As we praise together in our churches, we create a throne where God comes to dwell.

The reward of corporate praise is the manifest Presence of God.

Our singing attracts God. When He is pleased with our praise before Him, He comes upon our meetings.

Giving ourselves to worship and praise touches His heart to come and rest among us.

Singing praise is not a warmup for our heart to receive sermons. Singing praise is to touch His heart so that He will come and He will stay.

I love the way my church brings praise. All throughout the week we are lifting up praise.

He can't stay away from those who minister to and tend to His heart.

Corporate praise attracts the Presence. May we praise, so He comes, and may we keep praising, so He stays.

Lord Jesus, my King and my God! I love You! I love to praise You with the company of Your people that You would come and rest upon us. Help my church praise in such a way that You are enthroned upon us. In Jesus' name, amen.

Restore Us
October 23

Return to us, God Almighty! Look down from heaven and see! Watch over this vine, the root your right hand has planted, the son you have raised up for yourself. Your vine is cut down, it is burned with fire; at your rebuke your people perish. Let your hand rest on the man at your right hand, the son of man you have raised up for yourself. Then we will not turn away from you; revive us, and we will call on your name. Restore us, Lord God Almighty; make your face shine on us, that we may be saved.
Psalms 80:14-19

Do you have a personal bubble?

What I mean by that is, do you get uncomfortable when people get really close when they talk to you or hug you?

What makes it okay for someone to get close?

Of course, it's the people you love the most and are the closest to.

When someone you love and respect leans in to bless you and build you up with a message that they are pleased with you, it leaves you encouraged.

God draws near to us in His pleasure and His face shining upon us has the power to restore us. The Presence brings revival.

God's nearness has the power to restore and revive.

Revival is His nearness or the cause of revival is His nearness, according to Psalm 80. This Psalm repeats this phrase, "Restore us... make Your face shine on us."

This is a prayer and a cry for the corporate Presence, it's a promise for "us."

He comes on "us" in a way that He doesn't come on "me."

Revival comes in this Psalm when we are watched over by the Lord and when His hand comes upon the Son of Man at His right hand.

Revival is available to us because of Jesus, the Son of Man. He won't turn away our cries because of His Son. His face being near is a sign of His favor and the Son at His right hand is a sign of His favor.

When God comes near us corporately we have revival. As we come together in our churches let us lift up the Son of Man with cries for Him to revive us.

When He comes near and is manifest among us, His face shines and we are changed.

Anything is possible when His face is near.

O God, let Your face shine upon us and we will be restored! Let Your church lift up the name of Jesus the Son of Man. Let us experience the favor of Your face and the favor of Your right hand. Revive us and stay near us. In Jesus' name, amen.

Let's Go
October 24

I rejoiced with those who said to me, "Let us go to the house of the Lord."
Psalms 122:1

Whose house is your favorite place to go and have fun for a party?

My wife is a favorite for a party.

Before we were married, she was affectionately nicknamed the party thief by her friends because if she left one party for another location, people would leave with her.

Even now, after us being married all these years, she can gather a crowd.

Her nephew once made up a song that went, "Going to auntie's house, going to auntie's house..."

People are happy to party and celebrate with my wife.

King David starts out Psalm 122 that he is rejoicing with those who said, "Let us go to the house of the Lord."

There is a spirit of joy and celebration to go to God's house.

David is not just rejoicing alone; he is rejoicing with those who love to be in the house of the Lord.

The corporate Presence of the Lord comes upon us when we are together as God's people to enjoy Him.

There is a place for solemn encounters with the Lord, but there is also a place for us to gather in great rejoicing. Each corporate worship service ought to be a celebration of who God is to us.

We should have an excitement each week about coming together with the church for worship and celebration. We should have a sense of anticipation and excitement as if going to a party.

Our worship in the house of the Lord is an overflow of what God has done in our personal lives. Worship is a time of rejoicing where our lives and thanksgiving converge together as one sound.

Corporate worship is not a duty it's a delight for those who love the Lord and have learned to rejoice! Our corporate worship brings us joy because we love Jesus, and we love being with those who rejoice in loving Him too!

Our hearts are full when we hear some say, "Let's go to God's house!"

Lord Jesus, I love to worship in Your house with those who love You too! I rejoice in You! You are my delight. You are worthy of being celebrated. Thank You for Your people and getting to worship together. In Your name, amen.

The Commanded Blessing
October 25

Behold, how good and how pleasant it is For brethren to dwell together in unity! It is like the precious oil upon the head, Running down on the beard, The beard of Aaron, Running down on the edge of his garments. It is like the dew of Hermon, Descending upon the mountains of Zion; For there the Lord commanded the blessing— Life forevermore.
Psalms 133:1-3 NKJV

What do you think is something so attractive that it's almost magnetic?

Have you ever laid a trap to catch fruit flies or bees?

I've used peanut butter to trap mice many times.

For humans, in a positive sense, I think being kind is attractive.

I know that if I clean the dishes, I will attract praise from my wife. If my children listen to me and really take to heart what I've said, they will attract my favor. Of course, there are things we can do to make ourselves physically attractive to one another as well.

God is attracted to something in an almost magnetic way.

He is attracted to unity.

He cannot stay away from His people when we are unified together.

Unity attracts the Presence.

Unity brings the commanded blessing of the Lord.

In Psalm 133, David is sharing one of the most powerful truths about the corporate Presence of God in the Scriptures. When we live in unity, David says it is like anointing oil that runs down the beard and garment of Aaron.

Aaron was the high priest of Israel. Somehow, when we are unified as God's people, we have a priestly ministry. The high priest ministered to the Lord in His Presence.

This unity also brings God's blessing, like the dew of Hermon, upon the mountains of Zion. This dew brought fruitfulness.

When we are unified we touch the Lord's heart so that He blesses the fruitfulness of our lives. We encounter Him together in a way that we don't encounter Him alone.

He blesses us together in a way that He doesn't bless alone.

Unity causes us to live under the commanded blessing of the Lord.

Can you picture what that's like?

What kind of Presence and power is available to believers who unify in the name of Lord?

Is this not of the utmost importance that we love and honor one another in such a way that we can come together as one?

Do we want to be anointed, fruitful and blessed?

Coming together as a church with a single heart and single mind to love God and love one another creates an environment where God's commanded blessing comes upon us and we attract Him.

He can't stay away from our unity.

Anything is possible there in the Presence.

Lord God, let me live in unity with Your people. Let me love and honor my brothers and sisters in Christ. I want to dwell in unity that we might live under Your commanded blessing. Anoint my church like Aaron the high priest and make us fruitful, like the mountains of Zion. Do a supernatural work in us, Your people, as we unify in Your Presence. In Jesus' name, amen.

Worthless Assemblies
October 26

"The multitude of your sacrifices— what are they to me?" says the Lord. "I have more than enough of burnt offerings, of rams and the fat of fattened animals; I have no pleasure in the blood of bulls and lambs and goats. When you come to appear before me, who has asked this of you, this trampling of my courts? Stop bringing meaningless offerings! Your incense is detestable to me. New Moons, Sabbaths and convocations— I cannot bear your worthless assemblies. Your New Moon feasts and your appointed festivals I hate with all my being. They have become a burden to me; I am weary of bearing them. When you spread out your hands in prayer, I hide my eyes from you; even when you offer many prayers, I am not listening. Your hands are full of blood! Wash and make yourselves clean. Take your evil deeds out of my sight; stop doing wrong. Learn to do right; seek justice. Defend the oppressed. Take up the cause of the fatherless; plead the case of the widow. "Come now, let us settle the matter," says the Lord. "Though your sins are like scarlet, they shall be as white as snow; though they are red as crimson, they shall be like wool. If you are willing and obedient, you will eat the good things of the land; but if you resist and rebel, you will be devoured by the sword." For the mouth of the Lord has spoken.
Isaiah 1:11-20

. . .

Have you ever had someone share strong words of rebuke with you but also offer redemption?

I've had people rebuke me but be redemptive.

Words of discipline are not usually fun.

But to have someone who is strong in a rebuke also offer redemption is life giving. A warning can save your life.

I remember a pastor once telling me what his dad said when going to confront a family member who fell into sin and got pregnant out of wedlock. His dad said, "At times like this, we must act redemptively."

Thank God for people who love us enough to confront us truthfully and offer us redemption.

God spoke a strong rebuke through Isaiah the prophet to His people, Israel.

He said that He had "enough of their offerings," their "incense was detestable," , their assemblies were "worthless," their festivals He "hates," and His eyes "hide" when they pray their prayers.

All the things that are a part of the Presence being experienced corporately by Israel are now turning God away.

How can what attracts the Presence actually repel Him instead?

God said they had blood on their hands and that is why He was repulsed by their acts of worship.

God wants worship and devotion from a pure heart of obedience. He calls His people to seek justice and defend the oppressed.

How we treat the last and the least, the orphan and the widow, matters to God. We have to love humanity not only in word and intention but in our actions.

God doesn't want us to lift our hands in worship if they are dirty from oppressing the poor and disadvantaged.

But God promises cleansing of our sin if we come to Him.

He invites us in our sin and failure of loving others well to come to Him so He can wash us white as snow.

This is the gospel.

This is a Jesus promise that God invites us to Himself, where He provides the cleansing and purification of our sins so we can have clean hands before Him.

This is a warning and a promise to us as the people of God.

May we not only gather as the church for our own good, but may we be willing and obedient to love the overlooked in our churches and cities.

A church of the Presence not only burns the incense of prayer and brings the sacrifice of praise, but walks in obedience to caring for others.

———

Lord Jesus, thank You for washing our sins white as snow when we come to You with guilty and dirty hands. Let us love who You love and look after the least among us. Let us love justice for the oppressed like You do. Let us carry Your Presence to those who need You most. Forgive us for overlooking the needs of others. In Your good and loving name, amen.

Noisy Songs

October 27

"I hate, I despise your feast days, And I do not savor your sacred assemblies. Though you offer Me burnt offerings and your grain offerings, I will not accept them, Nor will I regard your fattened peace offerings. Take away from Me the noise of your songs, For I will not hear the melody of your stringed instruments. But let justice run down like water, And righteousness like a mighty stream."
Amos 5:21-24 NKJV

If you are a parent, do you enjoy the noise of your child practicing music?

Many parents may enjoy hearing their child practice, but some instruments can be rather difficult and loud to listen to, especially when a child is early in their training. I suppose drums could be annoying even if someone is skilled.

Your desire is peace and quiet.

I love hearing my kids play music and practice on their piano and guitars, but there are certainly times where I don't want to hear it; times when I need a break from *any* noise.

God loves praise and worship. That is clearly established all throughout Scripture.

The Psalms is a collection of one hundred and fifty songs of love and worship unto the Lord. This has been a major focus in a lot of my writings for the Presence, which makes this statement the Lord spoke through His prophet Amos even more shocking: "Take away from me the noise of your songs."

There are times when our corporate worship is just an annoying noise to the Lord.

This should be a sobering gut check for us as the church, and for church leaders. Similar to God's warning and rebuke in Isaiah, He is tired of our sacred assemblies, our offerings, our music, and our instruments.

We might have the most beautiful music and electrifying worship experiences, and God might not be anywhere near us.

How could this be?

The cry of God's heart is for our character and obedience to match our singing with righteousness and justice. This Scripture "Let justice roll down like water, and righteousness like a mighty stream" was a major focus of Dr. Martin Luther King Jr.'s famous *I Have a Dream* speech which made a huge impact on the civil rights movement in America.

This is the heart of our God.

We can't just sing while ignoring issues of righteousness and justice.

The prophets are full of cries for God's people to abstain from idolatry and sexual immorality, as well as turning from oppression of the poor and oppressed.

If our songs are being sung while our churches are full of sinful compromise and a lack of care for the disadvantaged, we are not truly honoring our Lord.

Let us be a church of the Presence and bring Him songs that are from a life of obedience, full of righteousness, and justice.

Lord and King, forgive us for bringing You songs that are not matched with obedience. Forgive Your church for where we overlook righteousness and justice. May we not only seek experiences with You, but our cry is that You would change us in Your Presence, so we will love and live like You. In Jesus' name, amen.

Walk Humbly
October 28

With what shall I come before the Lord, And bow myself before the High God? Shall I come before Him with burnt offerings, With calves a year old? Will the Lord be pleased with thousands of rams, Ten thousand rivers of oil? Shall I give my firstborn for my transgression, The fruit of my body for the sin of my soul? He has shown you, O man, what is good; And what does the Lord require of you But to do justly, To love mercy, And to walk humbly with your God?
Micah 6:6-8 NKJV

What do you give someone who has everything?

What do you give a king?

Do you think you should give someone with all the power something that shows your loyalty and heartfelt devotion?

I think giving a king a gift that displays honor is powerful, but ultimately, the gift you give a king should be the gift the king desires.

God desires three things from His people according to Micah 6: that we would do justly, love mercy and walk humbly with our God.

The prophet is speaking to the corporate people of God. They will not have the Presence by striving to bring the best sacrificial offerings of animals, oil, or even sacrificing their children.

God is looking to share His Presence with the people of God, as we have the right heart.

Justice, mercy and humility are all an invitation for us personally and corporately as the church to be a people of the Presence. The reward of these things is that we please the heart of God and in our humility, He walks with us.

Humility is a highway for the Presence of the King among us.

Our renunciation of self-reliance and our dependence on God in humility allows us to walk with the Creator of the universe.

This was Adam and Eve's experience of walking with God in Eden.

Justice, mercy and humility are a key to our original purpose of fellowship and companionship with God.

Our humility is seen in our posture before the Lord.

Our humility is also seen in how we love and care for others and stand up for the oppressed in justice and mercy.

Humility is not putting ourselves down, it's depending upon God and loving others well.

A people who practice these things will be a place where God dwells among us.

Lord of glory, I worship You! What am I to bring You? I so often love to bring you songs, but may my offerings be true and full of justice, mercy and humility. You are worthy of a just, merciful and humble people. May our worship be pleasing to You. In Jesus' name, amen.

Windows of Heaven
October 29

Yet from the days of your fathers You have gone away from My ordinances And have not kept them. Return to Me, and I will return to you," Says the Lord of hosts. "But you said, 'In what way shall we return?' "Will a man rob God? Yet you have robbed Me! But you say, 'In what way have we robbed You?' In tithes and offerings. You are cursed with a curse, For you have robbed Me, Even this whole nation. Bring all the tithes into the storehouse, That there may be food in My house, And try Me now in this," Says the Lord of hosts, "If I will not open for you the windows of heaven And pour out for you such blessing That there will not be room enough to receive it. "And I will rebuke the devourer for your sakes, So that he will not destroy the fruit of your ground, Nor shall the vine fail to bear fruit for you in the field," Says the Lord of hosts; "And all nations will call you blessed, For you will be a delightful land," Says the Lord of hosts.
Malachi 3:7-12 NKJV

Has someone ever blessed you for no reason other than to show you they loved you?

My friend Todd was like a big brother to me. He loved me and encouraged me all the time when I was a young man.

One time Todd knew I wanted a snowboard but didn't have enough money. He told me that he found a snowboard for one hundred dollars. I couldn't believe it. We went to get it and then I figured out he was buying over three-fourths of it. He loved me, so he blessed me.

When Israel had strayed from the ways of the Lord, God spoke through Malachi the prophet that if they return to Him, He will return to them.

The Lord promised the Presence if Israel would return. But they didn't know how to return.

The Lord's instruction about returning to Him is that His people no longer rob Him by not giving their tithes and offerings.

God is, in a sense, saying to Israel that if love Him, they will give.

The Scriptures are clear that we don't earn favor with God through giving for salvation or to experience His Presence.

However, a people who love God will be a generous people.

God promises the windows of heaven open over the corporate people of God who together bring their tithes and offerings to Him.

Financial blessing is only a part of God's blessing when His windows of heaven are open over us. The greatest blessing is that He is with us.

Again, this is not about earning our way for God to be near, it's the result of those who love God more than with just words but with their wealth.

God doesn't share His Presence with people who only give Him lip service. He doesn't want our songs if we won't give our heart.

We give our heart in relationship through giving of tithes and offerings.

God is a covenant making God, who is all about relationship with us.

A people who value this relationship will give to God out of love for His Presence, not to earn His Presence, but to give Him something of value because He is of the highest value to us.

Father God, thank You for the promised blessings for Your people who bring tithes and offerings into Your storehouse. Your Presence is our greatest reward of all. Let me and my church put You first in giving to show You our love. You are worthy of our best and our obedience. In Jesus' name, amen.

Among the Lampstands
October 30

I turned around to see the voice that was speaking to me. And when I turned I saw seven golden lampstands, and among the lampstands was someone like a son of man, dressed in a robe reaching down to his feet and with a golden sash around his chest. The hair on his head was white like wool, as white as snow, and his eyes were like blazing fire. His feet were like bronze glowing in a furnace, and his voice was like the sound of rushing waters. In his right hand he held seven stars, and coming out of his mouth was a sharp, double-edged sword. His face was like the sun shining in all its brilliance. When I saw him, I fell at his feet as though dead. Then he placed his right hand on me and said: "Do not be afraid. I am the First and the Last. I am the Living One; I was dead, and now look, I am alive for ever and ever! And I hold the keys of death and Hades. "Write, therefore, what you have seen, what is now and what will take place later. The mystery of the seven stars that you saw in my right hand and of the seven golden lampstands is this: The seven stars are the angels of the seven churches, and the seven lampstands are the seven churches.
Revelation 1:12-20

What is one of your favorite sounds?

One of my favorite sounds growing up (and still to this day) is the sound of rain or running water. I love it when raindrops get loud on the roof, a fountain or river is flowing, or even the sound of a shower.

I find the sound of water to be so relaxing and peaceful.

I used to position myself as a kid to be near the sound of water so I could hear it.

I have another favorite sound, the sound of God's voice.

There is a place to position yourself to hear the voice of the Lord. If you get near the Presence, you will hear His voice.

My Dad once heard a preacher go on and on about all the negative experiences he had in the church. He went on about the hurts, betrayals and pains he experienced by those in the church who mistreated him.

My Dad wondered where this guy was going with his message when he brought everyone to Revelation 1.

He said the reason he would never give up on the church was because that is where he can hear Jesus.

In Revelation 1, John writes Jesus is present among the lampstands and that the lampstands are representative of the church.

The voice of Jesus came from the lampstands.

John could see the voice which is mysterious.

This glorious, victorious and everlasting King dwells among the churches, and that is where He is heard.

Jesus is present in the corporate church in a way that He is not present with us individually. When we separate from the church, we separate from His body and the place where this glorious God—Man dwells.

Being with the church is to be near Him, and this positions you to hear His voice.

The voice of the Lord is heard in and through the church. This is not the only way Jesus speaks to us, but we will miss out on the fullness of His Presence and clarity of His voice if we cut ourselves off from His church.

Lord Jesus, I love Your voice. You are the Alpha and Omega, the One who was dead but is now alive forever and the One who holds the keys to death and hell. Heal any hurts I have from the church. Let me love the church like You do so I may be near You and hear Your voice. In Jesus' name, amen.

First Love
October 31

> Yet I hold this against you: You have forsaken the love you had at first. Consider how far you have fallen! Repent and do the things you did at first. If you do not repent, I will come to you and remove your lampstand from its place.
> Revelation 2:4-5

Have you ever seen an older couple that is deeply in love with one another?

I think it's wonderful to see newlyweds who are happily in love with each other.

Often, people will warn newlyweds that their honeymoon phase won't last forever.

There is some truth in that, because no one will have an easy life, yet I wish we would nurture romantic love more than discourage it.

But ultimately, a mature love that grows over decades and is evident to others is more powerful than young love.

Grace and I are blessed to witness both of our parents loving each other so well as they grow older.

We've been blessed in the church to see many other couples who love each other so strongly as they age, and it's beautiful.

Jesus is speaking to the seven churches in Revelation two and three. He has commendations and rebukes for these seven churches.

The first church He addresses is the church at Ephesus.

Ephesus had a powerful history. It was started in an outpouring of the Holy Spirit with the ministry of the apostle Paul. Paul started equipping disciples there, and the gospel spread throughout Asia Minor in two years so that everyone had a chance to hear the gospel.

Timothy, who was Paul's spiritual son, led the church after Paul. Church history reports that John the apostle attended there at the end of his life.

This was a dynamic church.

Jesus had a lot to praise Ephesus for and it appears they are the happening church in a lot of ways during this time period.

They were so mature that they were examining apostles to determine if they were true or false. They persevered and did good works. They did not tolerate evil.

But Jesus says they had one major problem: they left their first love.

They were "successful" according to the metrics of ministry, but they did not prize the Presence above everything else.

The church of Ephesus had lost the plot.

As a corporate church, our highest priority is to love Jesus more than anything else.

When we care more about success as the world counts it, more about prestige or more about appearing right than loving Jesus, we have fallen.

Jesus gave them a way back. He said they should repent and return to the things they used to do at first.

Do you remember the way you loved Jesus at first?

Do you remember how much you loved His Presence, worship and prayer when you first realized your sin was forgiven?

What about as a church together? Do you care more about ministering to Jesus and honoring Him, or do you care more about your own feelings and brand?

If we fail to love Jesus first as His church, what are we even doing?

It's sobering to realize that we can do much well, but if we don't love Him first and most, He will come and remove our lampstand.

———

Lord Jesus, thank You for Your love and zeal for Your church. Help us, Your church, to keep our first love in first place. In any way that we have fallen and turned from our first love, Lord, we repent and return to You. Help us return to the first things we did when we have loved You most. Awaken a passionate love in us for Your Presence. You are worthy of a people who love You first and love You most. In Your holy name, amen.

The Greatest Commandment

November 1

Jesus said to him, "'You shall love the Lord your God with all your heart, with all your soul, and with all your mind.' This is the first and great commandment.
Matthew 22:37-38 NKJV

Do you love tournaments?
    I love a good tournament.
    I grew up in a sports loving family.

My dad played in softball tournaments through a lot of my years growing up. I enjoy watching the playoffs in college and professional sports.

There was something invigorating or devastating about watching your favorite teams play, to see who would be the greatest. There is a desire in us to know who or what is the greatest.

Jesus taught in Matthew's gospel what the greatest commandment is.

He said the first and greatest commandment is loving God with all our heart, soul, and mind. That is the language of the Presence.

Life is ultimately about loving God. Everything we do ought to flow out of love for God.

Loving the Lord our God is the first and greatest commandment, not just because it's better than other commandments when you compare them head to head.

It's the greatest because it includes all the commandments.

When we love God the most, we are fulfilling all the other commandments.

We can't love God and lie or love God and steal.

If we are actively loving God with all of our heart, soul and mind, then we obey Him.

Being a person of the Presence is being a person who prioritizes loving God more than anything else.

What a great love this is with all of our heart, soul, and mind.

This immense love is a requirement because of God's greatness and worthiness. This is about our devotion and affection for Him over everything else.

God is worthy of love that is all in spiritually, emotionally and mentally.

Our worship, our study and our spiritual habits can all be used to help us cultivate a closer relationship and intimacy with God.

The way we conduct ourselves when we flee temptation, resist the evil one and obey the Scriptures should all be motivated by this great love for God.

Great and awesome God, my Lord and King, may I love You with all my heart, soul and mind! Let my love for You be first and most. Let my affection and devotion grow for You. There is no one like You who is worthy of all my love. Let my life be pleasing to You. I love You! In Jesus' great name, amen!

Pure Joy
November 2

Consider it pure joy, my brothers and sisters, whenever you face trials of many kinds, because you know that the testing of your faith produces perseverance. Let perseverance finish its work so that you may be mature and complete, not lacking anything.
James 1:2-4

What makes you the most joyful?
I would have to say, time with my wife and kids, especially if we are enjoying a great meal together.
Usually what brings us the most joy is time with people we love, a hobby we enjoy or performing well at a sport we play.
It takes an unusual person to find joy in some type of suffering or hardship.
James writes in his letter, that we are supposed to consider it pure joy when we find ourselves in various kinds of trials. Some translations say we should count it all joy in these times in testing in life.
People of the Presence learn to delight in God so much that they

become these unusual people who can rejoice when things are difficult in life.

James says these trials that test our faith produce perseverance in us. When we don't give up and persevere in trials, we become mature and complete to the point where we lack nothing.

I think most of us would like to lack nothing, but we don't typically enjoy this road to get there.

My dad has a little song he likes to sing when he finds himself in a test or trial.

He will sing when he preaches sometimes, too.

He sings, "It's working for me, it's working for me, it's working for my good. It's not against me, it's not against me, it's working for my good. This light affliction, it's working for me, it's working for my good."

Trials can make us bitter or better.

When we respond to God by trusting Him in trials, we can enter into joy.

Trials become a time where our illusions are broken, and we see where we really are. Trouble can cause the things that don't really belong in our lives anyway, to be stripped away, and we are left with pure joy.

Joy in trials is a key to living in the Presence.

Trials are not evidence that God is mad at us. Quite the opposite, trials are an opportunity to learn to rejoice in the Lord no matter what we endure.

———

Lord Jesus, I love You and rejoice in You! I choose to consider my trials and the testing of my faith pure joy! Help me persevere when things are tough, that You might have Your way in me. I want to become mature and complete, lacking nothing. Thank You for Your Presence in my trials. In Your great name, amen.

Tarry

November 3

> Then saith he unto them, My soul is exceeding sorrowful, even unto death: tarry ye here, and watch with me.
> Matthew 26:38 KJV

Are you familiar with the word "tarry?"

An evangelist told me he got to spend some time with the late Luis Palau who was a powerful evangelist in South America, the USA, and beyond.

He shared with me that when Palau was young, he and a partner would go into a city to do evangelism, but first they would go into a hotel room for around two weeks to tarry and pray.

As they stayed in that room, they experienced some type of breakthrough spiritually, where they knew it was time to evangelize.

And as I understand the story, without advertising or planning, they went out after that breakthrough came and start preaching where they felt led.

Then they continued to preach, and more and more people would respond to the gospel until hundreds and thousands of people came to faith in Christ.

He told my evangelist friend, "Your generation has forgotten how to tarry."

The word "tarry" in the Bible means to wait or remain.

The King James use of tarry seems to have some weight to it.

To tarry in prayer is not to be passive or lethargic. It's to spend time with Jesus, focusing on Him and ministering to Him.

It is a pressing in and yielding of the heart and soul to the Lord.

Jesus pleaded in the Garden of Gethsemane to his closest disciples - Peter, James and John - for them to tarry and watch in prayer with Him in His time of sorrow, when he was about to be betrayed and crucified.

He came to them later and lamented that they were unable to.

He then made an invitation that if they would watch and pray for an hour, they would not enter into temptation.

Jesus knew the power of the Presence, and waiting on the Lord or tarrying in prayer.

He knew that if they would tarry, they would not enter into temptation.

We don't like to wait much, though.

Prayer does not rigidly need to be an hour, but at the same time, we tend to want great results without any investment of time.

Our length of time in prayer, waiting on the Lord, does not twist God's arm or earn us special favor. But waiting on the Lord in prayer causes us to come to a place of trust, faith and agreement with God where we can pray from a pure place with the Lord.

We need to recover the word and practice what it means to "tarry" before the Lord.

If you want to know more of the Presence, then learn to tarry.

Don't treat God like a microwave or instant solution. Treat God as One to be known, loved and who is worthy of our time and devotion.

Those who tarry will experience great breakthroughs in themselves and in the prayers He leads us to pray.

Lord Jesus, teach me how to tarry in wonder and adoration. I want to pray not in a place of being rushed but from an active waiting where I pay attention to Your heart. I want to minister to Your heart in prayer in Your sorrows and in Your joys. In Your name, amen.

The Kingdom Belongs to the Kids

Then people brought little children to Jesus for him to place his hands on them and pray for them. But the disciples rebuked them. Jesus said, "Let the little children come to me, and do not hinder them, for the kingdom of heaven belongs to such as these."
Matthew 19:13-14

Don't you just love the way children can see things? Children have such incredible qualities of innocence, belief, and adaptability, and are quick to forgive.

Grace and I loved having children attend our wedding.

Children bring joy, vibrancy and some noise to our lives.

Our lives would be more orderly without children, but they would be much more boring.

Naturally, childish behaviors like fussing, selfishness, and acting out can be incredibly draining and stressful.

I remember hearing Bishop Joesph Garlington once share, "In the kingdom the key to maturity is not growing up but growing down to become more like a child."

According to the words of Jesus, this is so true. We are to develop a childlike faith.

When the disciples saw all the children coming to Jesus, they tried to get them to go away, but Jesus rebuked them and used it as an opportunity to share that we are to become like children to be people of the kingdom of God.

I heard another preacher once draw a powerful truth out of this Scripture.

What did the children see in Jesus that they would want to come close to Him?

If you know children, they are not flocking around an angry grump.

They probably wouldn't want to go to the disciples, and from what we see in the gospels, they also wouldn't want to go near the Pharisees, either.

But they loved Jesus. The way they perceived Jesus determined whether they would draw near to Him or not.

This idea applies a lot to our approach to God, prayer and the Presence.

If we don't see that Jesus is the clear picture to us of who God is, we don't want to go near Him.

Most people, when asked, think that God is mad or sad with them.

But if someone is often mad and sad, then you don't usually want to spend time with that person.

So, if we see God as more like the Pharisees or disciples, then we usually drift from prayer.

But if we remember that God is like Jesus, because Jesus is God in the flesh, we can see Him like a child and come in confidence and faith to enjoy Him.

———

Lord Jesus, I love You! Help recover my childlike heart and joy! I want to run to You and enjoy You as the children did. Let me see You as You really are! Let me see You the way children did when You walked this earth. Thank You, that I can come close and experience Your love and Your joy. There is no one like You! In Your name, amen.

The Greatest
November 5

At that time the disciples came to Jesus and asked, "Who, then, is the greatest in the kingdom of heaven?" He called a little child to him, and placed the child among them. And he said: "Truly I tell you, unless you change and become like little children, you will never enter the kingdom of heaven. Therefore, whoever takes the lowly position of this child is the greatest in the kingdom of heaven. And whoever welcomes one such child in my name welcomes me.
Matthew 18:1-5

How do you determine that someone is the greatest?
Do you measure their character?
Or is it their abilities?
Would you consider their appearance or their strength?
What about their intelligence?
Does charisma matter at all?
When it comes to sports, we can determine the greatest of all time (the GOAT) by someone's records, career wins or times.

But when it comes to a person in general, it can be hard to know how to weigh the different variables involved.

Jesus had an interesting measurement for who would be the greatest in the kingdom of heaven. He said that the greatest would be whoever takes the low position of a child.

Think about that.

The disciples are asking who is the greatest and Jesus takes a child to show them what true greatness is all about. He said we must change to become like children to enter the kingdom of heaven.

I love what G. K. Chesterton said here in his book *Orthodoxy* about how childlikeness captures the nature of God: "Because children have abounding vitality, because they are in spirit fierce and free, therefore they want things repeated and unchanged. They always say, "Do it again"; and the grown-up person does it again until he is nearly dead. For grown-up people are not strong enough to exult in monotony. But perhaps God is strong enough to exult in monotony. It is possible that God says every morning, "Do it again" to the sun; and every evening, "Do it again" to the moon. It may not be automatic necessity that makes all daisies alike; it may be that God makes every daisy separately, but has never got tired of making them. It may be that He has the eternal appetite of infancy; for we have sinned and grown old, and our Father is younger than we." *

Children like to explore and have an incredible curiosity. Their hearts are typically open to love, and they trust easily.

Childlikeness is the key to living in the kingdom and in the Presence. In fact, Jesus said that if we welcome a child in His name, we welcome Him.

Welcoming Him is welcoming the Presence, and we don't only do that by our worship and our prayers, but by welcoming a child in His name.

My wife and I love it when children worship. They dance and sing. They drop crayons and cereal everywhere. They run, laugh, clap and sometimes they cry or scream.

There is a place for solitude and silence before the Lord to enter His Presence in stillness, but there are also the colorful, messy, loud and expressive experiences that come along with worshipping Jesus with children, and like children.

Jesus, I love how You define greatness as childlikeness. Help me live in the simple trust and love of a child who belongs to You. Let me imagine and dream as a child. Let me love children like You do and welcome them so that You might be welcome among us. In Your name, amen.

Others and the Altar
November 6

"Therefore, if you are offering your gift at the altar and there remember that your brother or sister has something against you, leave your gift there in front of the altar. First go and be reconciled to them; then come and offer your gift."
Matthew 5:23-24

When you were growing up, did your parents get after you when you didn't treat your siblings right?

When I was growing up, I often remember my parents helping me (or making me) apologize to my siblings when I had done them wrong.

Of course, now that I am a parent, I do the same thing.

I think one of our top priorities as parents is to see that our children learn to love each other and get along. I mean, we are family, after all. Any sane parent desires to see their children learn how their words and actions can affect others, as well as how they should make things right when they have gone wrong.

Jesus loves us, His people, and God is a good Father.

As a Father, God desires His kids to get along. In fact, it is so important to Him that in the Sermon on the Mount, Jesus taught we should prioritize right relationship with one another before we enter the Presence. Jesus said we should not approach the altar if we remember that someone has something against us, but we first should reconcile before we come and give an offering to the Lord.

This does not mean that our human relationships are more important than our worship of God.

The altar represents the place of offering where we meet God in humility, repentance and obedience in our worship and where He communes with us by sharing His Presence.

It does mean is we shouldn't act spiritual like things are good between us and God while knowing we have offended someone else.

Here we see that the burden is on the believer who knows they have hurt or offended someone else. Elsewhere in Scripture, we are also told to go to someone if they have hurt us, to offer forgiveness.

The heart of God is that our human relationships are reconciled as much as we are able, because there is a connection between others and the altar.

We are spiritually deceived if we think we can mistreat others and have pure worship before the Lord.

God cares about His children loving one another as they profess to love Him.

God wants our relationships with each other to reflect the glorious relationship that He has with us through His Son, Jesus Christ.

Lord Jesus, thank You for all You have done for me to reconcile me to God. Let the Father's love fill my life by Your Spirit. Help me love others, honor them and reconcile with them when things are not right. May I humble myself to ask for forgiveness and to share it. Let my worship be pure before You, so You will receive my offering of love to You. In Your name, amen.

Ask, Seek, Knock
November 7

Ask and it will be given to you; seek and you will find; knock and the door will be opened to you. For everyone who asks receives; the one who seeks finds; and to the one who knocks, the door will be opened.
Matthew 7:7-8

What has been your most persistent pursuit?

Persistence is a very important trait to be successful in life, and persistence is also important in developing maturity.

I grew up playing a lot of sports, and often, whoever trains the hardest develops the most. Some people are gifted with unusual talent and genetics, but as Coach Tim Notke said, "Hard work beats talent when talent doesn't work hard." *

Stephen Curry has described himself as a basketball player that is not the strongest, tallest or the fastest.

So why is he one of the best players?

Because he is persistent in practicing, probably more than anyone else who plays the game.

Jesus said in teaching the disciples about who God is as Father in the Sermon on the Mount, that they should persist in prayer and in their pursuit of God. He said they should ask, seek, and knock.

The idea here is that whoever keeps on asking with be given to, whoever keeps on seeking will find, and whoever keeps on knocking will have open doors.

As a pastor, I see people give up quickly in the pursuit of God. Often, Christians who pray for the Holy Spirit baptism will pray one or two times, maybe three.

If they don't receive a prayer language in a few minutes or after a few attempts, they resign that God does not intend to fill them.

But I've seen others persist in asking, seeking and knocking sometimes for months and not give up. The ones who don't give up but keep pursing the Presence in their Christian walk, whether it's for Holy Spirit baptism or something else, amazingly receive the fruit of their persistence and God's goodness.

Often, Christians treat the Christian life like it's a math equation that can be solved quickly for each need or promise.

Or Christians can treat God like a cosmic vending machine.

But the Bible likens life to a war and God to a Father who loves us unconditionally. If you try to treat war or relationship like you treat equations, you don't usually get very far in either endeavor.

Don't get me wrong, God does not play games with us. We can trust His promises.

But He is teaching us here that we possess promises partially through asking, seeking and knocking (and, of course, by His grace and faithfulness ultimately).

Don't give up, Christian, in going after God in prayer and the things of the Presence. God may be forming maturity in you and has a purpose for you in pursuit of more of Him.

Lord Jesus, awaken in me a fresh hunger to ask, seek and knock until I receive, find and have open doors. Forgive me for where I have lost heart in Your promises. You have shown me a good picture of the Father and His heart to love me. Let me push past disappointment and persist in going after You wholeheartedly. In Your name Jesus, amen.

Presence Deception
November 8

"Not everyone who says to me, 'Lord, Lord,' will enter the kingdom of heaven, but only the one who does the will of my Father who is in heaven. Many will say to me on that day, 'Lord, Lord, did we not prophesy in your name and in your name drive out demons and in your name perform many miracles?' Then I will tell them plainly, 'I never knew you. Away from me, you evildoers!'"
Matthew 7:21-23

When you were growing up, did you ever enjoy seeing someone do illusions or "magic" tricks?

When I was growing up, I got really into learning how to do "magic" tricks.

Of course, there was no actual magic involved.

They were illusions.

What caught my interest was seeing magicians wow audiences and surprise people with card tricks, sleight of hand and making it look like things could disappear or appear out of thin air.

I never got that good at these tricks.

When some people get into doing tricks like this, things can also a take a turn towards the darkness of witchcraft type of magic. There is something in human nature that longs for the supernatural and the ability to bend reality.

Jesus had some strong words for people who treat the power and Presence of God as a place for almost magic abilities but who don't actually know Him.

Many charismatic and Pentecostal churches will often elevate those who can prophesy, cast out demons, and perform miracles. These are certainly important, valuable, and needed gifts in the body of Christ and the world.

But these are also the same gifts that Jesus warns about at the close of the Sermon on the Mount.

He tells those who call Him "Lord, Lord" they will not enter heaven and that they are evildoers.

This goes to show us that just because we could have supernatural power flow through us, we may not actually know the Lord.

This is a convicting reality about how we can be deceived about the Presence.

We can be around God's Presence and glory.

We can be in meetings and church services and places where God's power flows, and it can give us a false sense that we are truly right with God.

Being a person of the Presence is much more than an emotional experience or even a supernatural experience. Ultimately, being a person of the Presence ought to be a relational experience where we learn to know God.

I believe from other Scriptures that we should believe for the Lord to use us and even seek after prophesying, expelling demons and working miracles. But we must be a people that go deeper than the gifts and being around His Presence. We must be a people that truly know Him.

To know His Presence is to know Him.

———

Lord Jesus, keep me free from the deception of thinking I am more spiritual and more powerful than I really am. Help me to know You. May my desire be for You, and You alone. I love Your Presence because I love You. I love knowing You. There is no one like You. In Your name, amen.

Portraits of the Father
November 9

If you, then, though you are evil, know how to give good gifts to your children, how much more will your Father in heaven give good gifts to those who ask him!
Matthew 7:11

Who did you stay away from the most when you were growing up?

Let me guess.

You stayed away from grumpy, negative and mean people the best you could.

Even as adults, we usually like to stay away from critical and discouraging people.

Sometimes people are genuinely negative people, and sometimes it is our perception.

But either way, whether in reality or in our perceptions, we usually only want to spend time with people we enjoy being around.

In the Sermon on the Mount recorded in Matthew, Jesus is giving one of the most difficult teachings on human spirituality, morality and ethics. It's difficult in the sense that it's sometimes hard to live out these high standards.

The teachings are beautiful, inspirational but also very trying to love our enemies, forgive, be perfect, fast, pray, turn the other cheek when mistreated, endure persecution and more.

Sometimes, I didn't like reading the Sermon on the Mount because it reminded me of the areas I fell short in being Christlike.

One day, upon reading and reflecting on Matthew 5-7, I noticed the amazing ways that Jesus described the Father all throughout this passage.

I realized that when the focus was on me, the passage was heavy, but when I saw the Presence of the Father through these portraits Jesus creates of Him, I drew strength and knew He would help me:

PORTRAIT #1 - The Father is glorified when we shine our light (Matthew 5:16).

PORTRAIT #2 - The Father loves His enemies (Matthew 5:44-48).

PORTRAIT #3 - The Father is perfect (Matthew 5:44-48).

PORTRAIT #4 - The Father Rewards (charity) - secret works, open reward (Matthew 6:3-4).

PORTRAIT #5 - The Father Rewards (prayer) - secret works, open reward (Matthew 6:6).

PORTRAIT #6 - The Father Knows your needs (Matthew 6:8).

PORTRAIT #7 - The Father Forgives (Matthew 6:14).

PORTRAIT #8 - The Father Rewards (fasting) - secret works, open reward (Matthew 6:18).

PORTRAIT #9 - The Father Knows Your Natural Needs (Matthew 6:31-34).

PORTRAIT #10 - The Father Gives Good gifts (Matthew 7:11-12).

PORTRAIT #11 - The Father's will is a saving relationship with the LORD Jesus (Matthew 7:21).

The way we see God motivates whether we want to be in the Presence or not.

We often don't pray because we don't see God as someone who loves, forgives, and gives.

If we see Him as angry and grieved all the time, He sounds more like someone we don't want to approach anywhere in life.

As we see the Father through the Scriptures, our desire for Him grows.

———

Father God, thank You for giving me Your Son, Jesus. Thank You for being good and kind. You are generous and forgiving. Break off any false illusions I have of You. Let me see You for who You are. To really know You is to love You. I want to be near You. In Jesus' name, amen.

Don't Give Up
November 10

Then Jesus told his disciples a parable to show them that they should always pray and not give up... And the Lord said, "Listen to what the unjust judge says. And will not God bring about justice for his chosen ones, who cry out to him day and night? Will he keep putting them off? I tell you, he will see that they get justice, and quickly. However, when the Son of Man comes, will he find faith on the earth?"
Luke 18:1, 6-8

Do you remember things your dad told you growing up?

My dad was not only my dad, but also my pastor. So, I not only remember things he said repeatedly as my dad but also as a preacher.

He would often quote Winston Churchill's famous speech "Never give up, never give up, never give up! *

I've learned more recently that the speech may have gotten changed a little bit from "Never give in." But either way, we all need that reminder to never give up or never give in.

Sometimes we just need a dad or a friend to come and remind us to keep going.

Jesus encourages the disciples to pray and not give up, or as some translations say, not lose heart. He tells them a parable about a widow who went to an unjust judge repeatedly to get justice. The unjust judge did not fear God or care about others. But he got to the point where he said her persistence wore him out, so he gave her justice.

Jesus says to listen to what the judge says, and that God will give justice to His chosen ones who cry out day and night.

If persistence motivated the unjust judge, then how much more is our good Father motivated by our persistence?

We can get weary in prayer.

Even living in the Presence, which is often refreshing, can feel like we aren't progressing at times in the things we bring to our Lord.

Don't give up.

Don't give up or lose heart in prayer.

When we continue in prayer, we are bringing the Lord Jesus a gift of faith that He is looking for upon His return.

Persistent prayer demonstrates our faith.

Jesus is worthy of a people who don't give up in day and night prayer.

He will move to bring justice as we keep pressing in and we will bring Him what He desires upon His return, when He will be with us and we will be with Him.

Lord Jesus, You are good! You are coming back, and I desire You would find me contending in faith. Strengthen my heart in prayer. I won't give up. Day and night you are worthy of a people who seek You. In Your name, amen.

Mercy for Sinners
November 11

Two men went up to the temple to pray, one a Pharisee and the other a tax collector. The Pharisee stood by himself and prayed: 'God, I thank you that I am not like other people—robbers, evildoers, adulterers—or even like this tax collector. I fast twice a week and give a tenth of all I get.' "But the tax collector stood at a distance. He would not even look up to heaven, but beat his breast and said, 'God, have mercy on me, a sinner.' "I tell you that this man, rather than the other, went home justified before God. For all those who exalt themselves will be humbled, and those who humble themselves will be exalted.
Luke 18:10-14

Has there been a moment in your life that you were painfully aware of your need for God?

Some of our greatest breakthroughs in life come when we realize we are utterly helpless without the mercy of God. I've had several of these moments.

The voices of darkness and of this world would desire for us to see our neediness in a way that causes us to live in self-loathing and self-hatred. But when we see our true neediness before God and how we are desperate for Him, like we can really do nothing apart from Him and His mercy, we are going to receive a breakthrough.

Jesus taught in Luke 18 through a story about a Pharisee and a tax collector.

The Pharisee was a religious leader and scholar. He prayed out of self-righteousness. The tax collector was a sinner and despised by the culture. He prayed from a place of sincerity and contrition, "God, have mercy on me, a sinner."

Jesus went on to say that only the tax collector was justified in his prayer and that it is the humble who will be exalted.

When we come before the Presence, we need to remember that we are so needy for the mercy of God. Some Christians wallow in shame and self-hatred throughout their Christian life.

This is not what Jesus, nor I, am advocating for today.

But we never come to God on our own merits or because we perceive ourselves to be more righteous than someone else. That is self-righteousness, religiosity, and pride.

We never get to pray and come before the Lord on our own merits or earning.

We only come by His mercy.

A person of the Presence who is cultivating a prayer life ought to always walk in humility to seek God in mercy.

But in this kind of desperation, there should also be a confidence, because it puts our focus more on God, who shows mercy rather than our ability to hold ourselves up. True humility and repentance bring us into favor with God.

Bringing our weakness to God for mercy is not an act of weakness, but an act of strength.

God, have mercy on me, a sinner. In Christ's name, amen.

Good to Give Thanks
November 12

It is good to give thanks to the Lord, And to sing praises to Your name, O Most High; To declare Your lovingkindness in the morning, And Your faithfulness every night,
Psalms 92:1-2 NKJV

What is the greatest good you can do?

Well, I think saving a life is up there as the greatest thing you can do.

Only eternity will tell what was the greatest good that one did.

There are many good things someone can do, but there is one good thing you can do anywhere, at any time.

That is giving thanks.

It is always good to give thanks.

The psalmist of Psalm 92 was writing about the Sabbath day, a day of rest.

A day of rest every week was written in God's law and it's a great time to reflect and be thankful.

As often as we are able, my family spends time in worship, prayer and Bible reading each Sabbath.

We pray a blessing over our four children after we all take a turn thanking God for three things. It can be something from our week, our lives, or something we see in God that we give thanks for.

God is always worthy to be thanked!

He is not only worthy to be thanked but also to be thanked in singing.

He is the Most High!

There is no one higher or greater than Him in the heavens or on the earth.

Every day, we can declare His love in the morning and faithfulness at night.

There is always a reason to thank and praise our Lord!

It is always good to give thanks. In our trials, we can find things to be thankful for. In our joys, it is good to give thanks because we only achieve victory through His kindness.

In the morning and the evening, bring Him praise!

Not only is it good to praise because God is good, it is good to praise because it is good for us.

Thankfulness is good for our mental health and for our perspective.

Thankfulness is good for praising God and good for helping us.

Lord God, You are worthy to be praised! Thank You for Your loving kindness in the morning and Your faithfulness at night. I will bring You songs of praise. It is good to give You thanks! In Jesus' name, amen.

The Benefits
November 13

Bless the Lord, O my soul; And all that is within me, bless His holy name! Bless the Lord, O my soul, And forget not all His benefits: Who forgives all your iniquities, Who heals all your diseases, Who redeems your life from destruction, Who crowns you with lovingkindness and tender mercies, Who satisfies your mouth with good things, So that your youth is renewed like the eagle's.
Psalms 103:1-5 NKJV

At what age do people typically start thinking about benefits?

As a young man, I didn't care too much about my benefits at different jobs.

But then, as I was about to get married, my mom informed me I would be paying for my own surgery I had scheduled a few months before our wedding.

Then, benefits started becoming really important, and they became even more important when we had a baby shortly after our first year of marriage.

Your benefit package can make a big difference.

Dealing with insurance companies is one of my least favorite things to do in this adult life.

Getting the right benefits from a trustworthy source goes a long way to help you when you need it most and gives you more peace of mind.

God has a benefit package that is out of this world! And He is the most trustworthy source as our Provider of these benefits.

David starts Psalm 103 bursting with praise and thanksgiving. "Bless the Lord, O my soul."

Sometimes, you have to tell your soul to choose worship and thanksgiving when things are tough. An important part of the Presence is learning to praise Him even when you don't feel like it.

But in Psalm 103, David is overflowing with praise when he thinks of all the benefits of the Lord!

He is blessing the Lord for the benefits of being the One who:

forgives all of our iniquities (sins),

heals all our diseases,

redeems our life from destruction,

crowns us with lovingkindness and tender mercies,

and who satisfies our mouth with good things so our youth is renewed like the eagles.

God has a promise for every problem. Whatever we are facing, we can come to God for His redemption and His intervention in our lives.

Even when we are waiting for a breakthrough, we can choose to bless His name because He is the source of all that is good.

He forgives our sins, but He also heals us and redeems us from destruction. He is a promise giver and a promise keeper.

David was seeing ahead to the New Covenant promises of the Lord Jesus!

God cares for every need of our lives.

He is worthy to be blessed!

All good things come from His hand.

Bless His holy name!

Lord, I bless Your holy name! You are my Savior, my Healer and my Redeemer! You satisfy my mouth with good things, and You renew my youth like an eagle. You are my Source of all that is good. Thank You for the way You have loved me. May all that is within me bless You! In Your name, amen!

The Upright Shall Dwell

November 14

Surely the righteous shall give thanks to Your name; The upright shall dwell in Your Presence.
Psalms 140:13 NKJV

If you could live anywhere, where would it be?

My wife and I ask this question every once and a while.

Sometimes Grace likes to think about living in hot and dry cities in the Southwest because she loves how well her skin does in that kind of climate. But she usually decides she only likes to visit the desert and doesn't want to live there.

I love to visit warm places, scenic places and even cold places that are surrounded by the beauty of the mountains.

But when it comes to where we would dwell or live on a regular basis, we love the beauty of the Pacific Northwest. We both love the trees, the change of seasons, the rivers, the mountains and the ocean, which are all nearby.

David says in Psalm 140 that surely the righteous shall give thanks to God's name. The natural flow of the righteous is thanksgiving. The righteous in the Psalms are those who obey the Lord, love His Word and do good and not evil.

When our life is right, we ought to be thankful. If we notice thanksgiving is missing from our lives, something might be askew in our heart and character.

When righteousness has taken residence in us through Christ, then we ought to be thankful to the Lord and magnify His name.

The next truth that David connects in this song is that the upright (another name for the righteous) shall dwell in the Lord's Presence.

So, the righteous give thanks and they dwell in the Presence.

When our life is right, the outflow of thankfulness causes us to dwell with God.

The righteous live in God's Presence.

We don't earn our place in God's Presence, but we must never get flippant or casual with His manifest Presence.

He is present everywhere, as I have stated many times in this work, but only the righteous dwell in His manifest Presence.

We are righteous by faith in Christ, but if we truly have faith in Christ, then we will live an upright and righteous life.

The upright life of the believer is not one of perfection, but is a life characterized by obedience and repentance when we fall short.

If we want to dwell and live a life of depth in God's manifest Presence, then an upright and righteous life is not an option.

Even this standard of righteousness should not motivate us in pride, but ought to cause us to humble ourselves and come to God for His aid.

The righteous will be thankful and the upright get to dwell with Him! The Presence is the reward of the thankful and righteous!

Lord Jesus, thank You for Your righteousness that You have given unto me through faith in what You have accomplished. Touch my life with a holy conviction that I might be upright and dwell in Your Presence. My heart is full of thanksgiving and gratitude! You are worthy! In Your name, amen.

Thanksgiving Choirs
November 15

So I brought the leaders of Judah up on the wall, and appointed two large thanksgiving choirs. One went to the right hand on the wall toward the Refuse Gate.
Nehemiah 12:31 NKJV

Do you enjoy listening to choirs?

I've heard some incredible choirs in my lifetime. When choirs are done right, they add such a powerful dimension to music.

A large choir adds a sea of voices that creates an effect that nothing can replicate.

Choirs, especially in gospel music, add such a spirit of celebration and joy to worship. When a group sings, harmonizes, claps and moves together as one, a great sense of awe can inspire the rest of the room to enter into high praises.

Nehemiah had completed the rebuilding of the city of Jerusalem and re-instituted worship.

No rebuilding and revival is complete in the kingdom of God

without worship. The priests and Levites were set apart to minister unto the Lord once again.

This passage caught my attention recently, because Nehemiah appointed thanksgiving choirs. His heart and the people of Israel were so moved with thanksgiving that they had two entire choirs appointed to express how they felt.

When God does something great in our lives and churches, He is worthy of great acts of praise. He is worthy to be thanked and lifted up for the great things He does.

The Presence of God is not only something we experience alone in peace and quiet but it's also a corporate expression of thanksgiving.

Our thanks should be big and expressive. Our thanksgiving should move our church and our city and ultimately move the heart of God.

What could you, your family or your church do to bring God big praise?

How can you celebrate the things that God has done by bringing Him great expressions of thanksgiving?

Lord God, You are great and awesome! I celebrate You with thanksgiving! Let me live a life of great praise. Let Your church be extravagant and expressive in our praise for Your greatness. In Jesus' name, amen.

Joy Strength
November 16

They read from the Book of the Law of God, making it clear and giving the meaning so that the people understood what was being read. Then Nehemiah the governor, Ezra the priest and teacher of the Law, and the Levites who were instructing the people said to them all, "This day is holy to the Lord your God. Do not mourn or weep." For all the people had been weeping as they listened to the words of the Law. Nehemiah said, "Go and enjoy choice food and sweet drinks, and send some to those who have nothing prepared. This day is holy to our Lord. Do not grieve, for the joy of the Lord is your strength."
Nehemiah 8:8-10

Do you associate the word holy with joy?

I think if I'm being honest, I tend to think of the word holy as a somber word.

When I think of something that feels holy and joyful, I think of a birthday celebration. It's a day that feels special or set apart and joyful.

My parents, and now my wife, have always made it a special day.

But I think when it comes to days that are set apart as a holy day, we don't often think of them as joyful.

When Nehemiah was rebuilding the wall of Jerusalem, there was also a spiritual revival or return to the Lord.

Ezra the priest was leading this revival by re-instituting the reading of Scripture. Upon hearing the Scriptures being read aloud, the people wept after being deprived of them for so long.

Nehemiah had to tell everyone to stop crying on this holy occasion.

It was not a day for crying, but a day for rejoicing. Nehemiah proclaimed here, "The joy of the Lord is our strength!"

When we come before the Presence, we can have a single learned response that is more comfortable with tears than with joy and laughter.

But joy, rejoicing, and thanksgiving celebrations are also holy unto the Lord.

There is a place and time for tears and godly sorrow before the Lord's Presence. But it's important that we don't get stuck in one dimension of encountering God.

God is not only near us in our crying but He is near us in our laughter.

Holy days are not only days of fasting and mourning, they are days of feasting and celebrating.

The Lord is present in our celebrations and these times are holy to Him.

Celebration should be holy to us too. We are strengthened in the joy of the Lord.

Lord, Your joy is my strength. Thank You for helping me live in wonder, thanksgiving and rejoicing. Help me to not only fast but to also remember to feast and celebrate Your goodness. Release Your holy joy and the laughter and celebration in my life. In Jesus' name, amen.

ADORATION PRAYER
NOVEMBER 17

Ascribe to the Lord, all you families of nations, ascribe to the Lord glory and strength. Ascribe to the Lord the glory due his name; bring an offering and come before him. Worship the Lord in the splendor of his holiness.
1 Chronicles 16:28-29

Have you ever been in a prayer meeting that didn't really include much prayer?

One of my greatest pet peeves as a pastor is when there are prayer meetings without prayer.

I have been to a lot of prayer meetings where people taught, testified and socialized, but hardly had any actual prayer.

I like to say, "This is not a share meeting, it's a prayer meeting."

Of course, there are important times to teach, testify and talk with each other, but the most important words we are to utter are not to one another. The most important words we can utter are unto the Lord.

It's powerful to preach, but more powerful to pray.

It's one thing to speak to men for God, but it is quite another and a higher privilege to speak to God for men.

The greatest part of prayer is getting to speak to God about God and to adore His name.

Adoration prayer is the most important part of our prayer lives, where we lavish adoration upon the Lord.

King David, when he brought the Ark of the Covenant back to Israel, led into a prayer and song of adoration.

Adoration prayer in 1 Chronicles 16 is linked to the return of the Presence.

Adoration prayer is one of the greatest gifts for us to encounter the Presence of our God.

Adoration is all about thanksgiving and ministering to the heart of the Lord.

David was calling for people to ascribe glory to the Lord and to worship Him in the splendor of holiness.

Our adoration is when we don't just talk about God, but we speak to Him.

We thank the Lord and adore Him for His attributes.

It is a prayer of love and honor.

Adoration prayer is where we verbalize our fascination with God's beauty and character.

If you've ever been in a love relationship, then you know a little bit about adoration.

How encouraging is it when someone points out the reasons they love you?

We move the heart of God and draw near to His Presence when we praise Him and thank Him for who He is.

Adoration prayer is mostly focused on who He is.

I almost always start prayer meetings with adoration prayer and thanksgiving.

Adoration prayer fills us with faith as we meditate upon who God is to us and then praise Him for His glory and strength. As we lift Him up and adore His name, we sense His nearness.

———

Lord, You are worthy of adoration. There is no one like You. I ascribe to You glory and strength. I ascribe to You the glory that is due Your name. I worship You in in the splendor of Your holiness! I love You and worship You! Be near my King! In Jesus' name, amen.

His Love Endures Forever
November 18

Give thanks to the Lord, for he is good. His love endures forever. Give thanks to the God of gods. His love endures forever. Give thanks to the Lord of Lords: His love endures forever.
Psalms 136:1-3

Did you ever get told as a child that you had to say positive things about your siblings?

There have been some times in our family when one child gets negative about another. And one of our practices is that if someone is put down by their sibling, the one who did the put downs has to make a list of five or ten positive traits about their sibling to build them back up.

I'm not totally sure if this is effective or not, especially if the one who did the put downs is having a hard time finding a list of five or ten positive traits.

When we think of reasons to thank the Lord, we should be able to come up with more than five or ten reasons.

In Psalm 136, the psalmist cries out to give thanks to the Lord four times, three at the beginning and one at the end.

The main reason the psalmist gives is that the Lord's love endures forever. In fact, the phrase "His love endures forever" is repeated twenty-six times in this psalm.

Just the fact that the Lord's love endures forever should cause us to give thanks.

If His love endures forever, then God must have someone to love forever.

Life is not just earthly; it goes on forever.

Before life existed, God was present, and there was love within Himself.

His love with Himself as the holy trinity will last forever and be shared with all who have received His Son, Jesus Christ.

This revelation of everlasting and eternal love can only come from an understanding that Jesus the Messiah would come and make a way for us to enjoy God forever.

Remember that thanksgiving brings us into the Presence.

Because of God's eternal love, we always have a reason to praise.

The psalmist gives us so many reasons to thank God for His enduring love.

We thank Him because He is good.

He is the God of gods.

He is the Lord of lords.

He alone does great wonders.

He made the sun and moon.

He delivered Israel, God's people, from slavery.

He defeats our enemies.

He gives food to all creatures.

These are all evidence to us of His eternal love.

At times we might find it difficult to encourage or praise someone else for their good attributes, but God is so good and has done so many mighty things.

Use Psalm 136 in your pursuit of the Presence. You have dozens of reasons to thank Him for His enduring love.

Lord God, I thank You for the eternal love that endures forever because of Jesus. I thank You for being good. I thank You for being the God of gods and the Lord of lords. I thank You for all You have done for me and for Your many signs of love to me. I receive Your love. In Christ's name, amen.

The Spiritual Discipline of Thanksgiving
November 19

Devote yourselves to prayer, being watchful and thankful.
Colossians 4:2

What would you say is the most important spiritual discipline in your life right now?

If you are not familiar with the term spiritual discipline or spiritual practice, it is a term used to describe the habits that Christians cultivate in their lives to grow spiritually.

The spiritual disciplines are not a means of earning or striving, but are simply tools, graces and gifts which God has given us to renew our minds, develop spiritually, and grow closer to God.

The most popular spiritual disciplines are Bible reading and prayer. They also include worship, fasting, taking the Sabbath, silence, solitude, giving, serving, and more.

But, sadly, many Christians don't practice thanksgiving as an important spiritual discipline.

Now, most Christians who pray or worship regularly will most likely include thanksgiving in their time of prayer and worship.

And being thankful definitely belongs in those times.

We do also see repeated instruction throughout the Scriptures to practice thanksgiving. Paul said in the context of prayer to the Colossians that they were to be devoted to prayer in watchfulness and thanksgiving.

I believe our prayer times should be saturated with thankfulness.

It's not a bad idea to spend more time in prayer being thankful than asking for things.

I love what G.K. Chesterton said about being thankful: "I would maintain that thanks are the highest form of thought, and that gratitude is happiness doubled by wonder. When it comes to life the critical thing is whether you take things for granted or take them with gratitude."*

I agree thanks is the highest form of thought. A thankful life is a life caught up in God's wonder and a life lived in the Presence.

We can cultivate growth in thankfulness by making it a discipline.

A discipline does not mean there is no delight, but simply means to be intentional about it.

You could take a day of the week to focus on gratitude and thankfulness while you take a Sabbath rest.

You could write daily about one to three things you are thankful for in a gratitude journal like my mom.

Or like one minister I look up to, Doug String, you could spend two times in prayer every day. One to express gratitude and then, in a separate time, ask God for your needs and the needs of others.

Lord Jesus, let me develop of life of thanksgiving and gratitude. I want to be thankful every day. May my life overflow with gratitude for who You are and all You have done for me. By Your grace, I devote myself to prayer in watchfulness and thankfulness. In Your mighty name, Jesus, amen!

The Sacrifice at the End of Sacrifice
November 20

*Through Jesus, therefore, let us continually offer to God a sacrifice of praise
—the fruit of lips that openly profess his name.*
Hebrews 13:15

Who has sacrificed the most for you in your life?

Of course, if you are a Christian, the answer is Jesus.

But in other areas of your life, who has sacrificed the most for you?

Is it your parents?

Is it a spouse or a friend?

Have there been times when someone sacrificed money, resources, or time to help you?

What did you do to say thank you to that person?

The book of Hebrews is all about Jesus and that He is better than everything and everyone.

Jesus is better than the prophets, the angels, the priests, the sacrifices and the heroes of faith.

There is a major focus in Hebrews about how Jesus is the fulfillment of the Old Testament types and symbols of the prophecies, priesthood, and sacrifices. Jesus is both our High Priest and the ultimate sacrifice for our sins. Hebrews is clear that Jesus has completed everything He needed to do and His sacrifice for us on the cross is the end of sacrifice.

So what sacrifice do you bring the One who ended sacrifice?

You bring Him the sacrifice of praise, the fruit of your lips.

You tell Him thanks and you keeping telling Him thanks because He is worthy and He is wonderful.

The Old Testament believers brought sacrifices of bulls, goats, rams, and lambs. But because of Christ Jesus, we bring Him worship, praise and adoration through Jesus.

Our offering of praise is acceptable to God because Jesus' offering for us is always acceptable to God.

So, we come through His name and through His finished work on our behalf.

Through Jesus we experience the Presence every time we come through Him with praise. Singing our thanks for what He has done brings pleasure to His heart.

We can never exhaust His goodness in our lives.

Every time the church gathers, or we just wake up in the morning, He is worthy for us to bring a sacrifice of praise.

This is why we sing together and why we sing alone.

This is why we sing in the day and in the night.

This is why we sing now and forever.

This is why we sing on earth and why they sing in heaven.

We sing because of the cross where He has ended sacrifice for us and redeemed us to God.

Lord Jesus, I bring You a sacrifice of praise, the fruit of my lips. You have done it all for me. You have paid for my sins and redeemed me to God by Your blood. You have purged me from my sin, and I want to say thank You. You are worthy of all my worship. I exalt You in praise. There is no one like You. In Jesus' name, amen.

Who Loves Much?
November 21

"Two people owed money to a certain moneylender. One owed him five hundred denarii, and the other fifty. Neither of them had the money to pay him back, so he forgave the debts of both. Now which of them will love him more?" Simon replied, "I suppose the one who had the bigger debt forgiven." "You have judged correctly," Jesus said. Therefore, I tell you, her many sins have been forgiven—as her great love has shown. But whoever has been forgiven little loves little."
Luke 7:41-43, 47

Have you ever had a debt canceled?

We have tried to live debt free in our home as best we could, and mostly have, other than a home loan and some car loans.

There was a time when we had medical and dental debts stacked up.

It can be stressful to have debts when you are young parents, and you aren't sure how you are going to make ends meet or pay your bills.

When we got the news that our debts were canceled, it was such a joy that washed over us. It is an amazing gratitude that rises within you when you have debts paid by someone else or debts forgiven.

Jesus had a sinful woman come to Him in Luke 7 at a Pharisees house where He was dining. She anointed Jesus' feet with costly perfume and wept as she washed His feet with her hair and tears.

The Pharisees were appalled at this woman's act of loving devotion.

Jesus told the disciples this story above about two people who owed debts, one that was a small amount and one that was a great amount. So, when he asked them who would love the moneylender who canceled both debts more, Jesus said they rightly chose the one who was forgiven more.

Jesus used this story to illustrate that the sinful woman had many sins forgiven, so she had great love to show.

I used to think this story illustrated you had to commit a lot of sins and do some pretty bad things to love Jesus more. The more your past life was broken, dark, full of pain and evil, in my previous view, the more you could love Jesus once you were forgiven.

However, this meant that, in a sense, we would have to commit more sin and cause more harm in order to eventually love Jesus more.

After meditating on this story more, I realized we are all sinners who have equal need of Jesus.

This woman understood how great her sin was, so she loved Jesus much.

Sometimes, we think we have sinned so little, so we need little forgiveness. But this isn't true. We are all great sinners in great need of the Great Savior, Jesus Christ.

The key to loving Jesus much is to have a revelation that I have been forgiven much.

I love what I once heard John Piper say, "Every Christian has a great testimony because every Christian has been raised from the dead." *

My sin put Jesus on the cross, therefore it is a great debt that has been forgiven by Him.

I can encounter the Presence of Jesus in great ways, like this woman, in extravagant love, because I realize Jesus raised me from the deadness of my sin.

I always have a reason to love Him in thanksgiving and praise because of all He has done for me.

———

Lord Jesus, I love You so much! You paid the debt I owed so I could be forgiven and experience new life. There is no one like You! I come to You with extravagant love, for You have done a great work for me. My debt which was great has been paid in full by Your sacrifice. You are worthy of all my love. Thank You! In Your name, amen.

Gratitude Miracles
November 22

And one of them, when he saw that he was healed, returned, and with a loud voice glorified God, and fell down on his face at His feet, giving Him thanks. And he was a Samaritan. So Jesus answered and said, "Were there not ten cleansed? But where are the nine? Were there not any found who returned to give glory to God except this foreigner?" And He said to him, "Arise, go your way. Your faith has made you well."
Luke 17:15-19 NKJV

Have you heard the phrase, "Don't ask for more until you finish what you have?"

I think a lot of parents have probably said something like this.

It was the type of thing I would hear at the dinner table when I hadn't finished my food yet.

My parents taught me the importance of manners. I learned how to say please and thank you.

It's amazing how far gratitude and appreciation can get you in life.

My parents aren't the only ones who appreciate gratitude.

Jesus is moved by gratitude.

In Luke 17, Jesus was passing by when ten lepers cried out to be healed. He told them to go show themselves to the priests, and as they went, they were cleansed.

But only one of them, upon seeing He was healed, went back to thank Jesus and bow before Him.

Jesus acknowledged his act of worship.

This one thankful and former leper received some kind of wellness or wholeness (the KJV says he was made whole) that the others missed out on.

It appears all ten were cleansed and healed of their leprosy, but this man's gratitude released some kind of blessing the others missed out on.

And the greatest blessing was that He got to fellowship in the Presence of our Lord.

When we show gratitude and practice thanksgiving, we move the heart of Jesus.

Of course, we should come to Him with no agenda but to worship and thank Him.

But when we do, He loves to bless us and work miracles in our lives.

Gratitude releases the miraculous.

Whatever level of breakthrough or blessing we have received, we ought to thank the Lord and worship at His feet.

Being thankful brings us near Him, and anything is possible with Jesus.

For all that He has done, He is worthy of our praise and thanks.

May we come before Him with gratitude.

Jesus, thank You, thank You, thank You for touching my life and making me whole. I am grateful You cleansed me and called me to Yourself. I love You! You are the greatest thing in my life. I want to live for Your glory! In Jesus' name, amen.

Multiplication
November 23

And he directed the people to sit down on the grass. Taking the five loaves and the two fish and looking up to heaven, he gave thanks and broke the loaves. Then he gave them to the disciples, and the disciples gave them to the people. They all ate and were satisfied, and the disciples picked up twelve basketfuls of broken pieces that were left over.
Matthew 14:19-20

Have you ever witnessed a creative miracle?

I've seen some creative miracles where people experienced the restoration of their physical health or the mending of a broken part in their body.

But I've heard stories about people that have fed multitudes with a small amount of food (and I don't mean Bible stories, but stories from people who have these experiences in my lifetime).

I believe God can do anything, so I would marvel and be in wonder about God multiplying food or causing some natural force to change for His purposes of showing His love, power, and truth.

In Matthew 14, Jesus is healing people and a great crowd has amassed around Him (this story appears in all four gospel accounts of Jesus' life). In fact, there were five thousand men, plus women and children, who had gathered.

Jesus is so loving and good.

He was moved with compassion and wanted to feed the people.

But when he asked his disciples what food was available, they were only able to come up with five loaves and two fish from a young boy. Jesus took the loaves and fish and looked to heaven, giving thanks as He broke the bread. The food was multiplied to feed this large multitude, so much so that there were twelve baskets leftover.

Jesus shows us the key to miracles and multiplication in our lives: thanksgiving.

Gratitude has the power to work miracles.

As many preachers have said, "What is in your hand?"

Preachers share this because in the Scriptures, we see repeatedly that all God needs to do something great is what we have in our hand or what we have on hand.

God only needs our surrender with the little we have as we present it to Him with thanksgiving.

What could God do with the little that you have if you followed the model of Jesus?

We ought to develop a gratitude fixation.

Yes, I know very well that our circumstances often remind us we are so limited with the little fish and loaves we have on hand. We can often feel overwhelmed by insurmountable odds.

God specializes in doing His best works when we are outnumbered or under supplied.

Let us be thankful for what we have and present it to Jesus with gratitude. The blessing comes from what we bring to Him with gratitude in the Presence. When He is near, anything is possible.

Lord Jesus, I present to You what I have in my hand and what I have on hand with thanksgiving. Thank You for what I *do* have. I repent for the times I focus on what I don't have. I surrender to You all I am and all I have with gratitude. You are good! In Your name, amen.

Thanksgiving > Anxiety
November 24

Do not be anxious about anything, but in every situation, by prayer and petition, with thanksgiving, present your requests to God. And the peace of God, which transcends all understanding, will guard your hearts and your minds in Christ Jesus. Finally, brothers and sisters, whatever is true, whatever is noble, whatever is right, whatever is pure, whatever is lovely, whatever is admirable—if anything is excellent or praiseworthy—think about such things.
Philippians 4:56-8

Have you ever dealt with anxiety?

That's probably a silly question, because I would imagine everyone has.

When I got physically sick in my late thirties, I had severe anxiety as my health and strength dwindled.

I had dealt with anxiety to some degree before that, but I went to a counselor for some help when I was in crisis mode. Along with some reading by Dr. William Backus from *Tell Yourself the Truth*, I learned how anxiety causes you to rehearse things on a loop and "terribilize" events in your mind that usually never happen.

To "terribilize" something is to imagine that whatever you are thinking about will be terrible and play out in the worst ways possible.

I learned (and am still learning on some days) that I need to notice the pattern that anxious thoughts begin so I can stop and address my thought patterns with truth and thanksgiving.

Paul gives us a powerful antidote for anxiety.

He shows us that gratitude and thanksgiving have the power to combat anxious thinking.

Brain researchers and psychologists are, amazingly enough, talking about how thanksgiving has the power to transform our anxious heart and mind. We must recognize anxiety so we can choose in those times to "not be anxious about anything."

Then, in those moments, we can combat those negative patterns of thinking with prayer, asking God for our needs with thanksgiving.

Presenting our prayers with thanksgiving is the key to dealing with anxiety.

The power of the Presence manifests in God's present peace when we do this.

Beyond our understanding, God manifests His peaceful Presence in our lives as we give ourselves to prayer and His Presence.

He guards our hearts and minds because we are in Christ Jesus.

This is not a quick fix or earning our peace. Thanksgiving is accessing what Christ has already done for us to guard our hearts and minds.

Thanksgiving prayer will align your thoughts with God's truth and you will be protected in Christ.

We are then instructed to set our mind on true, noble, right, pure, lovely, admirable, excellent and praiseworthy things.

Whether we dwell in the peace of God's Presence depends more upon our mindset than it does our circumstances.

Thanksgiving is greater than anxiety.

Don't waste time on negative thoughts that will usually never occur.

Look to Jesus and His remedy of being thankful.

Lord Jesus, I exalt You with thanksgiving. Thank You for the cross and all You have done for me. I am in You. I am in Christ. I have peace with God through Your blood. Thank You for being with me in hard times. I reject anxiety as my lot in life, and I bring You my prayers and petitions today with gratitude and thanks. I set my mind on Your truth and on Your beauty. Guard my heart and mind. In Your great name, amen.

Not Contained
November 25

But will God really dwell on earth? The heavens, even the highest heaven, cannot contain you. How much less this temple I have built!
1 Kings 8:27

"How big is God and how tall is Jesus?" One of my cousins had this important theological question as a toddler.

So, my aunt called my dad since he was a pastor, and had her ask Uncle Dan.

I remember my dad being so happy about getting such a childlike question like this that inspired wonder and joy.

How come we don't ask these questions as adults anymore?

We have much to learn from children. A childlike perspective can cause us to live more in awe and wonder of our God.

A key to the Presence is staying fascinated with God.

The best prayer times I have are when I am fascinated with God.

The best prayers I hear in prayer meetings are people who exalt God and proclaim who He is with awe and fascination.

The best sermons I hear I leave me in amazement at who God is.

We need to live in astonishment at the grandness of who God is.

When Solomon was building the temple and bringing the ark into it, he prayed a prayer of dedication as recorded in 1 Kings 8.

This is where he prayed that "the heavens, even the highest heaven," cannot contain God.

Recognizing God's Presence at the Ark and the desire for that Presence in the temple, he noted God's existence is not confined to any building.

As I heard preacher Mark Brattrud say, "If the heavens cannot contain God, then God must contain the heavens." *

This thought is almost too wonderful for me.

God cannot be contained, yet He is near us and lives in us who are in Christ.

God cannot be contained in the heavens or in the earth, but He dwells in His church now as He did the tabernacle and temple.

He is so vast and so big that everything He has made cannot contain Him, rather, He contains all things.

He is so huge and mighty, but so close and so personal.

Why do we worry so much when all that we have and all that we are exists because of Him and is contained in Him?

If He made all things, then He is not contained by anything, but He contains all things.

We can't even get the full measurement of the universe.

He is a great God!

He is powerful, mighty and awesome!

There is no one like our God!

Father God, there is no one like You! You are the Creator and Sustainer of all things! You are the Almighty God. The heavens cannot contain You. You are greater than I imagined, yet You sent Your Son into this world so that I could know You. I marvel at Your greatness. In Jesus' name, amen.

Deny Yourself
November 26

Then Jesus said to his disciples, "Whoever wants to be my disciple must deny themselves and take up their cross and follow me. For whoever wants to save their life will lose it, but whoever loses their life for me will find it.
Matthew 16:24-25

Have you ever had the realization that your problems would go away if you weren't so selfish?

That can be a tough pill to swallow.

I think we have to examine that our selfishness can certainly be a root cause to the problems we face.

This applies to marriage, friendships, our careers and beyond.

I know it can be difficult to examine our own motives at times.

Our desire to blame others for our life choices and problems goes all the way back to Adam and Eve in the garden of Eden.

But there is true freedom when we let go of our selfishness.

Jesus said to His disciples that if we are disciples, true followers, we must deny ourselves, take up our cross and follow Him.

Truly following Jesus is a way of death, death to self.

Christ's message is so counter to the world that is all about self-expression and self-affirmation. We are told to express ourselves and be true to ourselves.

Yet Jesus says we are to deny ourselves.

Jesus gives us in incentive for following Him, denying ourselves and taking up our crosses to follow Him. That incentive is that when we lose our lives, we will save it.

The way of God's kingdom seems so upside down (but we are actually the ones who are upside down).

If we try and save our lives, we will lose it.

The path to the Presence is denial of self, death, and cross-like suffering.

We don't have to die for our sins on the cross. Jesus completed that. But His way was the way of suffering and self-denial, so to be like our Lord as His follower, we must do the same.

The call to follow Jesus is always first the call to be with Him, the call to the Presence kind of life.

I remember hearing Graham Cooke talk about how he wrote to a minister friend of his about all the ways people were hurting him, mistreating him and betraying him in ministry.

His mentor simply responded to his letters with the initials "D.Q."

It was short for "Die Quietly."

He would go on to say, "Die Quietly, no one wants to hear you scream."

We can feel like hardship, suffering and the cross we bear are not fair, or some kind of punishment.

But it's actually a privilege to be called on this path because it is the way of our Lord.

We are invited to walk like Him and to walk with Him.

He has not abandoned us in our suffering.

The things that come to kill the self-rule in us are actually helping us to lose our life so that we may find it.

Lord Jesus, thank You for bearing my sin and shame on the cross. Thank You for enduring suffering and being an example to me of self-denial. I lay down my life. I choose to follow You no matter what may come my way. I want to be with You and to be like You. In Your holy name, amen.

Suffering and Glory

But rejoice inasmuch as you participate in the sufferings of Christ, so that you may be overjoyed when his glory is revealed. If you are insulted because of the name of Christ, you are blessed, for the Spirit of glory and of God rests on you.
1 Peter 4:13-14

Have you ever met a Christian who has been persecuted for their faith?

I've had the honor of traveling to different nations to preach the gospel.

In one nation where I have ministered, the man who serves the leaders of the ministry has a missing hand and scar on his face. He is a joyful man and a faithful servant. When he put his faith in Christ, his own mother chopped off his hand and poured acid on his face.

Serving Jesus is his honor even amid the rejection of his family.

As my dad has traveled, he's met Christians who have been imprisoned and beaten for their faith.

One man, who was the most visibly joyful worshipper in some meetings he was in, would have his legs broken for preaching Jesus.

When his legs healed, he went right back and would receive beatings again.

His pain did not stop his joy and passion for Jesus.

In another nation, my dad met a man and would just weep because the Presence was so strong when he went near him.

My Dad couldn't speak his language, so he asked others why he was weeping so much around this man. They told him that this man was imprisoned and tortured for his faith.

Peter said in his first letter, that those who participate in the sufferings of Christ and are insulted for Him will experience the glory of God resting upon them.

We don't usually associate suffering with glory, but the cross has redefined for humanity what brings the glory of God.

The very things we suffer for Christ are the very things that draw the Lord near.

The Presence doesn't just rest on prayer meetings and worship services. The Presence also rests upon the believer that is imprisoned, rejected, insulted, slandered and tortured for the name of Christ.

We should not seek to suffer, but we should be prepared to suffer for Jesus for His ways of righteousness.

If He suffered and we follow Him, we can expect to be treated like Him.

We must remember the persecuted church as well and pray for them.

We have much to learn about the Presence from those who give up everything to follow Jesus.

The martyrs of church history often knew a deep intimacy with Jesus.

May we endure as they did until the very end with faith and love for our Lord Jesus Christ.

To suffer for Jesus is not a punishment but a reward that draws His Presence near.

———

Lord Jesus, I love You! Thank You for Your suffering. Thank You for the sufferings that I experience for Your name. Help me not to give up when I am insulted, rejected or mistreated for following You. Thank You for Your Spirit of glory and of God, that rests upon me in my suffering. In Your name, amen.

Overshadowed
November 28

Nevertheless, more and more men and women believed in the Lord and were added to their number. As a result, people brought the sick into the streets and laid them on beds and mats so that at least Peter's shadow might fall on some of them as he passed by. Crowds gathered also from the towns around Jerusalem, bringing their sick and those tormented by impure spirits, and all of them were healed.
Acts 5:14-16

Have you ever had or witnessed a supernatural miracle?

As of this writing, in the past few weeks we've heard testimonies in our church of a man in his seventies being healed of Parkinson's disease that's been verified by two doctors.

Another man with a flesh-eating disease and open sores is fully healed. The doctor thought after taking a few of his toes, they would have to amputate his limbs as well.

The doctor said he has never seen someone as bad as him have the disease reverse and experience a full recovery.

We've heard testimonies and seen people delivered of demons, other conditions healed, and people experience the power and filling of the Holy Spirit.

What is the key to experiencing miracles or letting God use you to work miracles?

The key is about the Presence.

The key is who overshadows you.

In Acts 5, God was doing extraordinary miracles through the apostle Peter.

The church was expanding as the Holy Spirit was moving, and Jesus was being preached. As more and more people were being saved, there was also a movement of healing taking place.

People would bring the sick and oppressed to lay them on beds and mats so that as Peter walked by, his shadow would release the healing power of God over them.

What a scene!

I wonder how many people were laying in a row on the ground, and as Peter walked by, what would it have looked like to see sick people getting up healed and impure spirits leaving the oppressed.

Peter's shadow could heal because he was overshadowed by the Almighty!

Peter had the mantle of Jesus, the Holy Spirit, who is, in fact, the same Spirit that all believers receive.

This happened because of God's manifest Presence.

Peter had a relationship with the Holy Spirit and the anointing of God was being passed from his life to those who needed a divine touch for healing and freedom.

As a pastor, I hear people say, "Why do I need to come to church to receive prayer? Why do I have to go to the revival meeting to experience God? God is everywhere. I don't need some healing meeting or healing minister to pray for me."

Where it's true that God is everywhere and able to heal us and hear prayer from any location, His manifest Presence makes a difference.

If people are healed under Peter's shadow, I don't think that's a time to be analytical about whether God is healing in other places. I would get in the shadow.

May we long for the Presence to overshadow us, that God may touch us and heal us, and that He may use us to carry His Presence to those who need His healing and freedom.

I want to get to the place where He manifests and bring others to Him too.

Lord God Almighty, thank You for bringing me near through Christ Jesus to dwell under the shadow of Your wings. In Your Presence is salvation, healing and freedom from impure spirits. Let me dwell with You and carry Your Presence to those who need miracles in their life. In Jesus name, amen.

The Grace of His Face
November 29

"Tell Aaron and his sons, 'This is how you are to bless the Israelites. Say to them: "'"The Lord bless you and keep you; the Lord make his face shine on you and be gracious to you; the Lord turn his face toward you and give you peace."'" "So they will put my name on the Israelites, and I will bless them."
Numbers 6:23-27

"Do you have gainers or drainers in your life?" I've heard my friend and mentor Leif Hetland ask this question in his preaching.

Are your relationships built with people who add gain to your life or who are a drain on your life?

We all have people that need help in our lives, and it would be wrong to cut them off if they drained us at any time.

The point is, though; we all need to have people who are gainers.

We need people and relationships in our lives who add grace to us.

We need people who, when we get around them, we sense we are loved and empowered to live for God and do great things for His glory.

God spoke something so powerful to Moses in Numbers 6. He gave

Him a blessing that Aaron and his sons were to speak over the children of Israel.

God not only gave Israel commandments, He gave them a blessing.

The blessing reveals His intention towards Israel to give them grace so that out of the Presence, they might be a people who obey their God.

This blessing is about the Presence.

This is about God blessing and keeping, making His face shine and being gracious, and turning His face towards them and giving them peace.

The blessing God gave them released the shine of His face, which brought grace and the turning of His face that brings peace.

This is a Presence blessing.

This is the favor of God: the nearness of His face.

When He is with us, we receive His grace and peace.

John Bunyan so beautifully said, "Run, John, run, the law commands, but gives us neither feet nor hands. Far better news the gospel brings: it bids us fly and gives us wings."

The Christian life through the gospel is pictured even in the Old Testament, and we see it here in Numbers.

God would supply grace to His people through blessing them.

His blessing changes us through that grace.

Grace empowers us and gives us wings to carry out what God says.

My wife Grace and I bless our children each week at family devotions with this blessing from Numbers 6. We want them to soar in the Christian life. We want them to associate our nearness with blessing and grace. Even more than that, we want our children to associate the nearness of God with His blessing and grace.

The Lord bless me and keep me, the Lord make His face shine on me and be gracious to me; the Lord turn His face toward me and give me peace. In Jesus' name, amen.

Build Yourself Up
November 30

But you, dear friends, by building yourselves up in your most holy faith and praying in the Holy Spirit, keep yourselves in God's love as you wait for the mercy of our Lord Jesus Christ to bring you to eternal life.
Jude 1:20-21

How is your physical fitness?

Do you enjoy doing cardio and strength training to improve your fitness, strength and health?

I enjoy doing physical workouts. I like the discipline and challenge, and I really enjoy seeing improvement. I do struggle to stay consistent over long periods of time.

Sometimes I workout for a few months, but then I hit a period where my training wanes.

One thing about working out is that there is no one else to blame when you fail to do it. You have to build yourself up.

At the end of this tiny book of the Bible, Jude says to build ourselves up in our most holy faith by praying in the Holy Spirit.

Of course, we receive the Holy Spirit by faith as a gift when we put our trust in Jesus, but we are to apply intention and obedience to building ourselves up by praying in the Spirit.

So many Christians believe that praying in the Holy Spirit here might be the gift of tongues or just praying with Holy Spirit's help in English or your first language. But if Scripture is the best interpreter of Scripture, where Paul says in 1 Corinthians 14, we pray with our understanding or in the spirit, then we should understand this to mean praying in tongues.

Tongues is a beautiful gift that allows us to pray in the Spirit, where the Holy Spirit prays through us.

Paul says in 1 Corinthians 14 that we speak mysteries when we pray in tongues.

In Romans 8, he says we pray the perfect will of God through the Spirit.

Jude says we build ourselves up.

Sadly, not all Christians speak in tongues. There are various theologies, but I hope beyond a debate you will see the invitation of the Scripture to have this gift operate in and through your life for your edification.

Jude is clear that we are to contend for the faith and have a strong theological defense for our beliefs earlier in his letter. But at the end he reminds us we need to be refreshed and built up in our faith.

We need the intellect, but we need the Spirit too.

Praying in the Spirit is a gift that strengthens your faith by allowing God to pray through you, enabling you to dwell in His Presence.

You have to choose to ask God for this gift, yield your tongue, and then, when received, you must engage with it.

Through praying in tongues, I have witnessed many believers, including myself, experience the love of God, conviction of sin, courage for witnessing, tenderness towards others, a love for Scripture, hearing God's voice more clearly and the flow of other spiritual gifts.

Building yourself up by praying in the Spirit is not a selfish act, it renews you so that you might glorify God and minster to others well from a place of refreshing.

Jesus, I honor You, my Savior and Lord, as the Baptizer in the Holy Spirit and fire. Fill my life and release or renew the spiritual language of tongues in my life. I want to pray in the Spirit, build up my faith and keep myself in the love of God. In Jesus' name, amen. (Wait on the Lord to speak in new tongues if you have asked sincerely or ask another believer to pray with you and pray in the Spirit).

Advent

December 1

But with the precious blood of Christ, a lamb without blemish or defect. He was chosen before the creation of the world, but was revealed in these last times for your sake.
1 Peter 1:19-20

When does your family set for Christmas?

Christmas is coming soon; do you have your Christmas decorations out yet?

People have strong feelings about when Christmas decorations should go up in and on a house. I always thought setting up for Christmas after Thanksgiving is over was a good time, but now for some it is getting even earlier.

My grandpa grew up in a home that didn't set up anything for Christmas until Christmas Eve. That's right, there were no Christmas decorations, a Christmas tree or presents sitting out.

My grandpa would wake up when he was a boy on Christmas morning and come out to see a tree, decorations and all sorts of gifts.

His parents stayed up all night setting up a tree and putting up lights to get ready for Christmas Day. It might have all come out on one night, but they had to be very prepared for what was coming.

In Peter's first letter to the church, he talks about the redemption we have as believers and that our redemption is through the precious blood of Jesus. This is the blood of the Lamb of God, who is without defect or blemish.

Then Peter says He was chosen before the creation of the world but was revealed in these last times. He is talking about the first coming of Jesus, which is the incarnation, where Jesus came in the flesh.

This coming of Jesus, the Lamb of God, is also celebrated by the Christian church from the first Sunday of December through Christmas Eve, as Advent.

Advent means "coming" in Latin.

This coming is all about the Presence of God coming to us in Christ.

Jesus came to be born of the Virgin Mary two thousand years ago. This is what Peter is referring to as "these last times" when Christ was literally revealed by taking on human flesh.

Although Jesus came, and it was announced to Mary and Joseph, it was actually before the beginning of creation that Jesus was chosen to come for us.

This was not God's plan B.

Jesus' coming and eventual death on the cross, where His blood was shed as the Lamb slain for us, were not an emergency reaction to the sin of humanity.

God knew when the world was formed, God the Son would have to come for us, as a man. He came fully human but was (and is) fully God.

God knew that for us to be near Him, to have fellowship and a relationship with Him, He would have to come.

This is the key to understanding how the entire Bible ultimately reveals Jesus, the Lamb of God.

The whole Bible story is one great story that is preparing us for His coming.

This time of Advent leading up to Christmas is to look at His coming and remember that He is coming again to be with us forever.

Lord Jesus, Lamb of God without blemish or defect, thank You for Your precious blood. You were chosen to come for us before the foundation of the world. What love You have shown us. Open my eyes to the power of Your advent and Your incarnation. Help me see how much You desire to be with me. In Your precious name Jesus, amen.

Incarnation
December 2

The gospel he promised beforehand through his prophets in the Holy Scriptures regarding his Son, who as to his earthly life was a descendant of David, and who through the Spirit of holiness was appointed the Son of God in power by his resurrection from the dead: Jesus Christ our Lord.
Romans 1:2-4

Have you ever thought about what it would be like to time travel?

The interesting thought to me about time travel would be experiencing a different world or culture.

Even visiting America hundreds of years ago would probably seem very unique.

Visiting Europe over a thousand years ago would be even more strange.

How would you interact with people?

How would you explain where you came from and what the world is like in their future?

Advent is the time where we celebrate Christ's coming, which is His incarnation. He, being eternal, entered into time and space to be a part of our world.

Jesus was not created when He was conceived of the Holy Spirit in His mother Mary. Jesus was and is eternally God, the second person of the Trinity.

Jesus entered our world and into human history, being fully God and fully man.

I love how Bill Hogg once put it: "Jesus is God as if He was not human and Jesus is human as if He was not God at the same time without contradiction." *

Paul says in Romans 1 that the Son of God in His earthly life was a descendant of David and through the Holy Spirit, He was appointed the Son of God in power by His resurrection.

This is Jesus: He was already the son of God but took on an earthly life.

He came from another dimension. From heaven to earth, from eternity into time and from a glorious body to a fleshly one.

Paul connects the incarnation to the resurrection.

In fact, Jesus first coming and incarnation is always connected to His life, death, burial, resurrection, and second coming for which we await.

Saint Athanasius said, "And thus He, the incorruptible Son of God, being conjoined with all by like nature, naturally clothed all with incorruption, by the promise of the resurrection." **

Jesus, becoming like our nature in the flesh, the Son of David, joined us to His incorruptible nature, making us sure of resurrection.

In the art of the early church, there was a connection between the tomb and the womb.

Jesus' incarnation has brought life to our death and out of His death, He brought life to us.

Remember, the Presence is His person being near.

Jesus created the opportunity for us to know Him in a living relationship by reconstituting the world through His incarnation. He came to live as us, so we could know Him, and we could become like Him to be with Him forever.

Jesus, thank You for taking on a fleshly body, becoming God incarnate. You brought Your life to transform our death. Thank You for Your Presence here among us so that I could know You and be with You now and forever. Precious Lord Jesus, in Your name, amen.

The Seed
December 3

So the Lord God said to the serpent: "Because you have done this, You are cursed more than all cattle, And more than every beast of the field; On your belly you shall go, And you shall eat dust All the days of your life. And I will put enmity Between you and the woman, And between your seed and her Seed; He shall bruise your head, And you shall bruise His heel."
Genesis 3:14-15 NKJV

Have you ever been around people that like to "talk trash" in sports?

If you have never heard the phrase "talk trash," it means to insult and mock your opponent and to brag about how much better you are.

Sometimes people like to talk a lot in sports or a competition to gain a psychological edge over their rival. Many times it's out of insecurity or to make up for their lack of skill.

One thing I love to watch is how my wife likes to "talk trash" to my dad (and others) when we play various kinds of games as a family. Even if my wife is losing by a huge amount in something, by the way she talks, you would think she is about to annihilate my dad or other opponent.

Of course she does it in a spirit of fun.

But when someone talks this way for real, it gets pretty embarrassing if they can't back it up.

At the very beginning of the Scriptures, after Adam and Eve sinned against God when they listened to the serpent, God told His adversary that one day He would destroy him.

God, of course, wasn't "talking trash" because He knows the end from the beginning.

He wasn't even making a prediction; He was making a prophecy. This prophecy is that a Seed (or Child) was coming from woman that would crush the serpent.

Yes, the serpent would cause the Seed a little pain but would ultimately be destroyed.

This is the story of the Bible: Jesus would come, born of a woman named Mary, and He would destroy Satan, His enemy.

The Bible says this is the purpose that Jesus came, to destroy the works of the devil (1 John 3:8).

The Presence of Jesus here meant the destruction of Satan, our greatest foe.

Christmas is good news in great part because it was the destruction of Satan's head and the ruin of His kingdom.

It was the plan of God from before creation began that Jesus would enter this world in His incarnation. It was announced right after the fall of humanity in Adam and Eve's sin.

God already had a remedy planned for the first humans living below their true inheritance of walking in the Presence of God.

It appears that Satan attacked the patriarchs' wives and other key women of Scripture through barrenness.

Those who had a promise from God, like Abraham and Sarah, could not conceive a child after receiving a promise that God would make them great in the world.

Often, the places we are most attacked could be our greatest areas of promise.

But one thing was for sure, when God promised a child, they always came.

And when God promised Jesus all the way from the beginning, although it took many generations, His Presence among us caused destruction of Satan's kingdom.

———

Father God, thank You for the promised Seed, Your one and only Son Jesus. He was manifested to destroy the devil and all His works. Thank You for Your promises in my life that Satan Himself cannot stop. In Your Presence, the evil one is thwarted. I rejoice in Your promise and victory. In Jesus' mighty name, amen.

Immanuel
December 4

Therefore the Lord Himself will give you a sign: Behold, the virgin shall conceive and bear a Son, and shall call His name Immanuel.
Isaiah 7:14 NKJV

What kind of answer do you think you would get if you asked people what the greatest problem in the world is?

Yes, even if you asked conspiracy theorists.

I think people would say things like the economy, government corruption, wars or racial and ethnic hatred.

If you asked people who are concerned about the environment, they would probably say global warming, climate change or a lack of natural resources.

If you ask the truly poor of the world, they would probably say hunger or the lack of access to food.

I guess it depends on where you live and what you are facing in some ways, but I believe the greatest problem the world faces is that people live without God.

In Isaiah's prophecy about the Messiah, he says the Lord will give His people a sign that the virgin will be with child and bear a Son who will be called Immanuel.

This is what Christmas and the incarnation are all about, God being with us. That is what Immanuel means, "God with us."

Our greatest need as humanity was for God to be with us.

God could visit His people in a cloud, in fire, in His tabernacle, or even come upon people by His Spirit for specific tasks and assignments He had for them. But Jesus, the Son of God, being born to the Virgin Mary, was God coming to be with us.

What do we need for our pain? God with us.

What is the hope of the nations? God with us.

What brings us peace and joy? God with us.

What are we missing as a result of sin? God with us.

What can reverse the curse of the darkness in our present age? God with us.

Jesus being called Immanuel means Jesus is "God with us."

God with us means the Presence.

Jesus is the Presence.

Jesus coming to the earth in His incarnation, is how God is with us.

Jesus becoming a man changed how God could dwell with us.

He doesn't visit us anymore; He is with us.

He became as us so He could be with us, and we could be with Him.

Being a person of the Presence is simply about beholding Jesus.

Knowing, loving, and adoring Jesus causes us to dwell with Him.

This is why He came, to be with us.

He is Immanuel. He is God with us.

———

Lord Jesus, I worship You. Thank You for taking on human flesh to come and be with us so that I could be with You. You are God with us. I praise You Immanuel! This Advent season, allow me to learn the power of simply being with You. In Jesus' name, amen.

A Child is Born
December 5

For to us a child is born, to us a son is given, and the government will be on his shoulders. And he will be called Wonderful Counselor, Mighty God, Everlasting Father, Prince of Peace. Of the greatness of his government and peace there will be no end. He will reign on David's throne and over his kingdom, establishing and upholding it with justice and righteousness from that time on and forever. The zeal of the Lord Almighty will accomplish this.
Isaiah 9:6-7

What is your favorite thing about God?

It can be hard to answer that question because once you get to know who God is, you know there is so much to love about Him.

Many Bible preachers and teachers have accurately said that the most important thing we can think about is who God is. How we see God will determine how we see ourselves, how we see the course of our life, and how we see the events of history unfolding around us.

A main part of the reason Jesus came to the earth was to show us who God is.

Isaiah's prophecy in chapter 9 reveals something about this amazing Lord that we love and serve. Jesus, this child, the Son of God and the Son of man, born to us, will be called Wonderful, Counselor, Mighty God, Everlasting Father and Prince of Peace. The government will be on His shoulders, and He will establish everlasting peace.

He is multi-faceted and awesome in His nature.

He is all we need.

He is Wonderful. That is He is full of wonder. He is awe inspiring.

He is Counselor. We can ask Him anytime and wisdom pours forth from His mouth.

He is Mighty God. Jesus is fully human, but He is also Mighty God. He is fully divine and powerful.

Jesus is Everlasting Father. This is not to be confused with Him being God the Father. Rather, He is the second Adam and started a whole new people as the head or Everlasting Father of all of us who have believed on Him.

He is the Prince of Peace. He rules with peace and His rule established peace.

He is the Prince, the highest authority of peace on the earth.

The peace of Jesus will have no end because His government will be established across the whole universe. This began with Christ's first coming, where His kingdom was inaugurated on the earth. But it will be established completely at His second coming when His kingdom is consummated.

This Child that was born had authority, the government is on His shoulders.

But as Isaiah says, He will one day reign on David's throne from Jerusalem. He will conquer at His second coming all His foes, every demon and devil, and even death will be abolished.

His kingdom government will cover the entire new heavens and new earth where He will rule in peace forever and ever.

The Presence of this King means peace for the whole world, and in Him is all we need.

The Wonder of the Presence

Lord Jesus, I worship You! You are Wonderful. You are Counselor. You are Mighty God! You are Everlasting Father! And You are Prince of Peace! There is no One like You. Your rule and kingdom establish peace and have no end. In Your great name I pray, amen.

The Shoot
December 6

A shoot will come up from the stump of Jesse; from his roots a Branch will bear fruit. The Spirit of the Lord will rest on him— the Spirit of wisdom and of understanding, the Spirit of counsel and of might, the Spirit of the knowledge and fear of the Lord— and he will delight in the fear of the Lord. He will not judge by what he sees with his eyes, or decide by what he hears with his ears; but with righteousness he will judge the needy, with justice he will give decisions for the poor of the earth. He will strike the earth with the rod of his mouth; with the breath of his lips he will slay the wicked.
Isaiah 11:1-4

Have you ever felt like you were judged unfairly in a competition?

My children compete in a speech and debate league. Their education is centered on being in a speech and debate club, and they compete in tournaments throughout the year.

The judges determine who wins or loses.

They can do their best, but if a judge has a unique value system or doesn't understand the rules, they may get judged in a way that is not fair.

No one likes to be judged unfairly.

In Isaiah 11, God is speaking through Isaiah about the coming of Jesus the Messiah.

He will be the Shoot that comes from the stump of Jesse. Jesse is the father of David. David was the greatest King of Israel and the prophecies about the Messiah are that He would come from the line of David.

But here He comes as the descendent of Jesse, which means He will be like David and superior to David.

The stump means that things look bad, the tree has been cut down, but the Shoot will come forth and from the roots a Branch will bear fruit.

Jesus will restore what has been lost and be the perfect King and Judge over humanity.

How is Jesus, the Shoot, better than David as King?

He has the sevenfold Spirit of God upon Him: The Spirit of the Lord, of wisdom, understanding, counsel, might, knowledge and the fear of the Lord.

He will not judge according to natural wisdom, what can be seen or what can be heard, He will judge righteously. His kingdom will be known for true justice and righteousness.

He will uphold the poor and the needy.

He will judge the wicked.

Jesus came as a little Shoot out of the disappointment of the past kingdoms in His incarnation, but He would grow into the Branch bearing fruit.

He would be anointed with the Holy Spirit.

He came lowly to touch the lowly.

He has come and He will come again.

When He returns, He will judge the wicked who are proud.

His judgement will be perfect.

The Presence of Jesus came to bring hope and peace as the Son of David.

When He comes again, He will establish perfect righteousness and justice.

———

Jesus, You are the Shoot and the Branch and my life is found in You. Upon You is the Spirit of the Lord, of wisdom, of understanding, of counsel, of might, of knowledge and the fear of the Lord. When You are present, there is perfect judgment and justice. Help me treat others like You and not judge on outward appearance. In Your name, amen.

Glory Revealed
December 7

A voice of one calling: "In the wilderness prepare the way for the Lord; make straight in the desert a highway for our God. Every valley shall be raised up, every mountain and hill made low; the rough ground shall become level, the rugged places a plain. And the glory of the Lord will be revealed, and all people will see it together. For the mouth of the Lord has spoken."
Isaiah 40:3-5

Have you ever met someone and had a certain sense of who they are, but discovered there was so much more to them than you originally thought?

When I asked a mentor and eventual fellow minister, Scott Smith, about my girlfriend (who is now my wife), he told me there was so much more inside of her that was going to blossom over time.

You see, I had been inquiring about Grace to Scott, because he knew her for a long time. I was trying to figure out if she was the right one for me.

I knew what he said was true. She was the most beautiful, joyful encourager I had ever met.

I have discovered over the years that her talents, gifts and abilities far exceeded even what I knew about her when we were married. She has exceeded all my high expectations in every way.

Isaiah prophesies about one who will come before the Lord and prepare the way for His coming. He will be a prophetic voice. This verse would be fulfilled in John the Baptist.

He came before Jesus.

This prophecy from Isaiah seems to be twofold and have implications for Jesus' first and second coming.

Isaiah said "the glory of the Lord will be revealed".

It was revealed in some form, in Jesus' first coming, but His second coming will be the fullness of God's glory revealed.

There is so much more to this child being born than what first appeared.

When Jesus was born on Christmas Day, His glory was revealed through the shepherds, when He was seen in the temple by Simeon and Anna, and when He was a child to the magi who visited Him.

But this humble baby born to a faithful Jewish couple would literally alter the landscape of human history.

His incarnation meant the beginning of events that would lead to His death, burial, resurrection, ascension and return.

Jesus coming will mean that valleys are raised, mountains are brought low, and rough and rugged places made smooth.

Jesus revealed the Presence, the glory of God.

His Presence, or glory, revealed in His birth and life events, will be an increasing glory that fully culminates upon His return.

In His first coming, God was present among us, and He remains present by His Spirit.

But when He comes again, we will experience His Presence forever and this will establish a new order for the world that is ruled by our King who makes wrong things right.

Lord Jesus, You have come, You will come again. How I long for Your return. Your glory has been revealed, but I want to know Your glory more and more. You will make all wrong things right. I look forward and pray for the day when You will reveal Your glory in all Your fullness when You come again. In Your great name, amen!

O Little Town of Bethlehem
December 8

But you, Bethlehem Ephrathah, though you are small among the clans of Judah, out of you will come for me one who will be ruler over Israel, whose origins are from of old, from ancient times.
Micah 5:2

Have you ever overlooked something because it seemed insignificant?

We often judge things by their outward appearance and books by their covers.

But big things are often hidden in small packages.

We rarely know when our life is going to change or what God is going to use to get our attention. Sometimes the most unexpected people, places or situations will have the greatest impact on us.

We see people counted out in sports or in life when they don't fit the normal mold of what looks successful.

God loves to choose foolish and overlooked ways to accomplish His great purposes.

When Jesus, our Immanuel, God with us, came to the earth, it was through the humble and righteous Virgin Mary.

But this was not the only way that Christ's coming or Advent may have seemed foolish. Jesus was not born in a palace or in a great capital city.

He was not born in a place with great connections and networking opportunities through his education and community.

God chose to be born in the little town of Bethlehem.

Bethlehem was a small town a few miles from Jerusalem. It was small among the clans of Judah, but God chose for this humble small town to be the place where the ruler over Israel would be born.

The Lord speaks through Micah that the Messiah, who is the ancient one of old, the eternal One, would come to a humble little place. The Presence would come in an unexpected and overlooked place. This was not the center of culture, education, government, or religion.

It was just a small town not far from significant places.

As people of the Presence, we must remember that God can meet with us and manifest anywhere. He can meet us in a church conference with passionate worship, or He can meet us in the most beautiful chapel under a steeple. But He often chooses to manifest Himself in unexpected and forgotten places.

No matter where we are at, God can meet us there and show Himself to us.

We are never hidden before the Lord.

I've met with God after being on a boat with my friend.

I've met with God in my closet and in living rooms.

I've met with God walking by the river or when I was hugged by a child.

I've met with God in what seemed like small and dry prayer meetings.

Bethlehem reminds us not to count out the small or insignificant places or seasons in our lives.

Don't judge things by their initial appearance, for you may very well be somewhere unexpecting that God is about to appear.

Lord Jesus, Whose origins are of old from ancient times. You are the ruler of Israel. You who came meek and humble from Bethlehem but rose to change the world as King of kings and Lord of lords, remind me not to count out the humble beginnings and insignificant places in which You choose to manifest. In Your precious name, amen.

Come Away

December 9

My beloved spoke and said to me, "Arise, my darling, my beautiful one, come with me. See! The winter is past; the rains are over and gone. Flowers appear on the earth; the season of singing has come, the cooing of doves is heard in our land.
Song of Songs 2:10-12

What is one of the worst parts of dating?

I know you might have different answers to this question, but to me the worst part of dating Grace before we were married was having to drop her off at night and drive home alone.

One of the best parts of marriage was getting to finally be together at night and not go our separate ways.

The drive home alone while dating just left a greater longing for me to be with her and look forward to marriage.

Advent readings don't always include a Scripture from Song of

Solomon, but I believe it's very fitting because it has to do with a longing to be together.

What is Advent, but a time to long for the coming of Christ.

We remember what led up to His coming and we long for Him to come again.

The Song of Songs (or Song of Solomon) is about King Solomon and His young wife. This book is a love poem between these two young lovers from their courtship to their marriage, and even has a lot to say about their physical intimacy.

Some see the Song of Solomon as an allegory between Christ and His church. This is because of the connection that Paul and John make by connecting Jesus the groom with the church as His bride.

While I believe we should not overlook the practical and romantic aspects of this book being about a marriage, it has to have something to say for us because of this connection between Christ and His bride. After all, if the whole Bible is pointing to Jesus, then even this romantic love poem has something for us to see about Jesus.

Advent, the coming or appearing, is all about the Presence.

We long for the Lord to come and be with us and also, He longs to come and be with us.

In Song of Songs 2, the groom is speaking to the bride: "Come with me. I want to be with you. I want to share life with you and your beauty. It is time for the singing of songs."

This is the language of longing to share life, relationship and intimacy.

Not only do we long to be with Jesus and wait for His return, He longs to be with us and come to us again.

Singing is an act of worship to the Lord Jesus, but it is also a way we connect with His Presence until His return, when He can be fully present with us forever.

During this time, I hope you will hear His voice saying to come and be with Him.

He longs to share His life with you.

Jesus, King and Groom, I love You! Let me hear Your voice calling me to be with You. I long to be with You and You long to be with me. Thank You for this love relationship You have brought me into by Your grace. There is no love like Your love. Come Lord. In Your name, amen.

Redemption of Our Brokenness
December 10

This is the genealogy of Jesus the Messiah the son of David, the son of Abraham.
Matthew 1:1

What does your family tree tell you?

Looking over a family tree can provide a variety of emotions. There can be a mixture of pride and honor to sadness and shame.

A family tree tells stories of heroes, but also of broken promises and great pain.

A family tree can also give you an understanding about yourself and how you got to where you are today.

Matthew begins his gospel letting us know the history of Jesus' family. It begins with His genealogy.

It's actually not a complete genealogy, but it was written to show that Jesus was the Son of David and a descendent of Abraham, since Matthew was written primarily for a Jewish audience.

We get to see the history of Jesus' family leading up to the Presence of Jesus entering history in His incarnation.

Through the genealogy in Matthew 1, almost all the names listed are fathers and sons.

But there are a few names that make an unusual appearance: Rahab, Ruth, and Uriah's wife.

These are interesting names to place in Jewish genealogy because Rahab and Ruth were not Jews. All three of them were broken women who went through hardship or mistreatment in some way.

They had a past.

They are not the kind of women you think would be placed in a family tree, especially when so few women were listed amongst the dozens of men.

But this is exactly why their placement is so powerful.

Jesus' Presence changes the most broken stories.

Christmas is not a story of Jesus coming into a family line of perfection, but a family line of redemption.

God can use the most broken people for His most glorious purposes. Christmas and the holidays can magnify the brokenness of our families.

Don't underestimate what being a faithful person of the Presence can accomplish in your family and in your generational legacy.

You might not always see God's redemption in sudden miraculous things, but through the consistent faithfulness and obedience of your life, you can see God bring restoration to your family.

Jesus changed everything for humanity.

He still changes lives and gives meaning to our stories.

His Presence can make the broken whole and bring redemption to the hardest situations.

Lord Jesus, thank You for my family. Thank You for the power of Your redemption. No one can bring beauty out of brokenness like You can. Let Your Presence touch the lives of my family during the holidays. Let us see Your goodness in our family tree. In Your name Lord, amen.

Costly Christmas
December 11

When Herod realized that he had been outwitted by the Magi, he was furious, and he gave orders to kill all the boys in Bethlehem and its vicinity who were two years old and under, in accordance with the time he had learned from the Magi.
Matthew 2:16

Have you noticed how busy Christmas has become in America?

Christmas shopping, Christmas parties and Christmas decorations can be fun and memorable, but can also fill our lives with so much stress.

Finding the right gift can be meaningful, but it can also be costly and inconvenient.

I think all the hustle and bustle of this season can simply be due to good old fashioned greed and ignoring God's rhythms of rest.

But it can also be a reminder of the first Christmas; that when God shows up, it's not always in the midst of comfortable and convenient times.

After Jesus is born and around age two, wise men or Magi, from the East, come to visit Jesus.

King Herod discovers their plan to visit Jesus, who they are calling a King. He is threatened by the birth of Christ and seeks to deceive them so he might kill Jesus.

God delivers a plan to the Magi and to Joseph and Mary so they can escape for their lives.

But Herod kills all the two-year-old boys and younger in the area of Bethlehem.

Mary and Joseph have to flee for their lives to Egypt for a season.

Then they will have to move to Nazareth later on.

Mary already had the cost and inconvenience of being a virgin carrying a child. This would appear as immoral and indecent for her and Joseph to be engaged with her being pregnant.

It was costly for Jospeh to stick by Mary and not divorce her.

It was inconvenient for both of them to go to Bethlehem during a census while Mary is pregnant and then have no place to stay.

After all, Jesus was born in a manger.

Christmas came at a cost to everyone involved and especially to Jesus Himself, who left His comfort and glory of heaven to become incarnate as the Son of Man.

We don't often get to experience the Presence when everything is easy in life.

We have to prize Jesus' Presence above the cost of inconvenience in our lives.

We might picture that our encounters with God's Presence come when we are on vacation, in a worship service with our favorite band, or when the right type of people pray for us.

But often Jesus shows up in our lives when we overlooked, threatened, unsure and desperate.

The good news is that Jesus can show up whether we feel like it or not. He shows up in the midst of stress and trials, not based on whether or not we deserve Him. We can respond and obey even when things are hard.

Although we may struggle, when He comes, the Presence of our King makes it all worth it.

Lord Jesus, no matter what cost I might pay or however inconvenienced I am, You are worthy of my all. Thank You for showing me how to look for You to manifest beyond my feelings or stress levels. Your Presence is my highest prize. I love when You come near. In Your name, amen.

Light Power
December 12

In him was life, and that life was the light of all mankind. The light shines in the darkness, and the darkness has not overcome it.
John 1:4-5

What usually wakes you up in the morning?

Is it your alarm clock? Your spouse or your child? Is it a rooster or a pet?

I am awakened by a variety of things in my busy life.

But one of my favorite things to be awakened by is when my wife pulls back the curtains of our bedroom windows and the light of the sunrise bursts into our room.

Our bedroom window faces the sunrise that comes up over the mountains. On a clear or partially clear day, the sunrise is breathtaking.

It can hurt my eyes a little to go from darkness to light so quickly, but when my eyes adjust, the light displays the beauty of the sky, mountains and valley.

John chapter one is a more mystical and theologically rich explanation of Jesus' incarnation.

When we speak of Advent and His coming, we often rightfully think of the story of Mary and Joseph.

But John doesn't focus on this part of Jesus' life. He begins his gospel with the manifestation of Jesus as "the Word."

He says that in "the Word" was life and His life was the light of humanity.

This "light shines in the darkness and the darkness has not overcome it."

The coming of Jesus, the Word in the flesh, was an overcoming victory for the light over the darkness. When Jesus took on our humanity and came to dwell among us, it was a defeat for the kingdom of darkness.

St. Athanasius wrote extensively on this in his work, *The Incarnation of the Word of God*. He mostly refers to Jesus in his book as the "Word of God." He links the coming of Jesus with His death and resurrection that all together lead to a decisive victory over darkness.

In His coming, Jesus has overcome the darkness of our sin, our sickness, evil spirits and false gods.

Translators differ on describing the light "overcoming" the darkness.

Sometimes they say something more like the darkness has not "comprehended" or "understood" the light.

The darkness had no idea what was happening to it when the Son of God came in the flesh.

Light always wins.

No amount of darkness can put out the light, but light always shines in the darkness.

When we are in the Presence of Jesus, we are in the Presence of the light.

Darkness and evil have been defeated and are no match for the God-Man our Lord Jesus Christ. He has the power to deal with any darkness.

When we come before Him, He shines on us and reveals places to turn from sin, receive His healing and His freedom.

But not only does He show us where we need to change, His light is a power that performs the operation we need to change and be whole.

King Jesus, Light of the world, Word of God, shine on me. Drive out all darkness from my life. Your coming meant utter defeat of all darkness. I want to live in the light and warmth of Your Presence. Let Your light shine in me and through me. Be glorified in me. In Your holy name, amen.

The Name Jesus
December 13

This is how the birth of Jesus the Messiah came about: His mother Mary was pledged to be married to Joseph, but before they came together, she was found to be pregnant through the Holy Spirit. Because Joseph her husband was faithful to the law, and yet did not want to expose her to public disgrace, he had in mind to divorce her quietly. But after he had considered this, an angel of the Lord appeared to him in a dream and said, "Joseph son of David, do not be afraid to take Mary home as your wife, because what is conceived in her is from the Holy Spirit. She will give birth to a son, and you are to give him the name Jesus, because he will save his people from their sins."
Matthew 1:18-21

Do you know the meaning of your name?

My friend and co-worker in the gospel, Andre Benjamin, often asks people if they know the meaning of their name.

Not a lot of people know their name's meaning, but he rightly encourages them that there is a powerful truth behind it.

This often helps people see their life's purpose or even opens their heart to God.

I believe in God's common grace in the world and He directs parents to give names that even they are unaware of at times.

God connects your life purpose to your name, and it's worth finding out.

The birth of Jesus, as we've been discussing, was a history shaking and universe altering event because God became incarnate in the flesh.

In Matthew's gospel, we see some of the supernatural activity surrounding this miraculous birth of Jesus the Messiah.

The Lord appeared to Jospeh in a dream.

Joseph had been considering putting Mary away because of the apparent scandal of being engaged to a woman who was pregnant.

But the Lord comes to Him to say He has chosen Joseph to be the father of Jesus because Mary is pregnant by the Holy Spirit.

Jospeh receives this honor, as well as the instruction to name this Child, Jesus.

The name in the Hebrew for Jesus is Yeshua.

Yeshua is the name Joshua and means Yahweh, the Lord, saves.

The name Yeshua is directly connected to the Lord's message in the dream that this will be His name because He will save His people from their sins.

The Name encompasses who He is.

His birth and incarnation, His Presence among us, will always be connected to His name. The Presence is always connected to the Name, the Name of Jesus.

In the name of Jesus, Yeshua, is our salvation from sin, Satan and death.

There is power in His name.

As we proclaim His name and pray His name, we experience His Presence.

In His Presence, we are saved and made whole.

He came to save us from our sins so we could know Him and our fellowship with God could be restored.

There is no one like Yeshua our Messiah!

Lord Jesus, Yeshua my Messiah, my King and Savior, I praise You! Thank You for coming. Thank you for Your Presence. You have saved me from my sins, and I am eternally grateful. There is power in Your name, my Lord. I love You above all others! In Your mighty and all-powerful name, amen!

Overshadowed
December 14

"How will this be," Mary asked the angel, "since I am a virgin?" The angel answered, "The Holy Spirit will come on you, and the power of the Most High will overshadow you. So the holy one to be born will be called the Son of God... "I am the Lord's servant," Mary answered. "May your word to me be fulfilled." Then the angel left her.
Luke 1:34-35, 38

What is your favorite type of gift for Christmas?

Growing up, I hated receiving clothes as Christmas gifts.

One side of my family gave clothes pretty much exclusively, and the other gave mostly toys.

But as I got older, I liked receiving clothes more and more.

Now that I am an adult, the thing I like the most about Christmas is time in the presence of the people I love. Relationships have become more important than things, but of course, I still enjoy a gift, too.

The first Christmas came to be because of the most radical Presence encounter in history.

The Virgin Mary, whom God had chosen to be the mother of Jesus, was visited by the angel Gabriel. Gabriel said she would bring forth a Son, but she was not sure how this would take place since she was a virgin.

Gabriel said it would be by the Holy Spirit, Who would overshadow her by the power of the Most High.

Mary had one response to the Presence encounter that the angel prophesied over her about: "May your word to me be fulfilled."

Eve received a prophecy after losing the Presence in Genesis that a Seed would come forth born of woman.

Eve disobeyed the word of God to her.

Mary is the fulfillment of Eve's prophecy.

She obeyed the word of the Lord.

Mary demonstrates the right response to encounters in the Presence, where we are overshadowed by God's Spirit.

We still experience these encounters with the Holy Spirit.

Our response in these moments ought to be like Mary, "Yes and amen! Have Your way in me, Lord."

There is no other response to experiencing the Holy Spirit.

God's response to our response of obedience is to bring miraculous works about in and through our lives.

Mary was chosen specially as a humble and holy woman who obeyed the Lord.

He trusted His eternal purposes to Mary and her soon to be husband Joseph.

When the Holy Spirit comes upon ordinary and humble people who trust the Lord, great things are possible.

When God overshadows His people, His Presence changes history.

———

Father God, thank You for the obedience and example of Mary. Overshadow me with Your Spirit. I want to encounter Your Presence and have a heart that says, *"May Your Word be fulfilled in me."* I love the work of Your Presence. Be near me and birth great things in my life. In Jesus' name, amen.

The Forerunner
December 15

There was a man sent from God whose name was John. He came as a witness to testify concerning that light, so that through him all might believe. He himself was not the light; he came only as a witness to the light.
John 1:6-8

Have you ever had someone go out of their way to make a way for you?

One of the best feelings in life is to have someone believe in you and go out of their way to help you succeed in what you need to accomplish.

My friend Ben Dixon is like that; he goes out of his way to give me opportunities in ministry because he believes I have an important message to share.

He invites me to his church, his conferences or his podcasts and encourages people to get behind me.

All of us ministers ought to follow his example to lift up others to help them succeed.

In John 1 where we learned about Jesus being the Word and the Light, we learn that there was a man named John who came to be a witness of the light.

John here would later be known as John the Baptist.

As the story goes, John is a relative or cousin of Jesus, who was born shortly before Jesus. He was born to come as the forerunner of Jesus.

He was to go before Jesus and make a way for the message of Jesus by proclaiming His identity and mission.

John is clear about this forerunner, John the Baptist.

He is not the light. But as He goes before the Light as a witness to testify of Jesus, all might believe in Him.

God raised up John the Baptist to go before Jesus and testify to who He is.

He was a man sent from God.

He was man of the Presence.

He lived a peculiar life.

He was a man on fire with God's purposes.

He was the last Old Testament prophet.

Jesus' Presence coming to the earth came with one final prophetic voice to confirm His identity and mission.

The prophets all point to Jesus.

The prophets point to Jesus so that we might know Him and experience relationship, fellowship and His divine Presence.

We only know Jesus through the revelation of the prophets.

There was a historical record of God's Word confirming who Jesus would be as the Messiah.

As great as the Light is, He still chooses the voice of the forerunner to be a witness to who He is.

And those who've encountered the Presence, forerunners sent even now, carry His message to those who'll one day accept Him as Lord.

People of the Presence are sent to testify and prepare the way for the coming move of God and ultimately for the return of our precious Lord Jesus.

What a privilege to be a voice who goes before another, but not just any other, the Lord Jesus Himself.

May our lives not be about promoting ourselves but about promoting Him.

———

Lord Jesus, I want to be a forerunner like John. I want to go before You and testify of You. There is no one like You, great Light of the world. Let my life burn with a passion to make You known and proclaim who You are so that others might encounter Your Presence too. In Jesus' name, amen.

Joyful Womb
December 16

At that time Mary got ready and hurried to a town in the hill country of Judea, where she entered Zechariah's home and greeted Elizabeth. When Elizabeth heard Mary's greeting, the baby leaped in her womb, and Elizabeth was filled with the Holy Spirit. In a loud voice she exclaimed: "Blessed are you among women, and blessed is the child you will bear! But why am I so favored, that the mother of my Lord should come to me? As soon as the sound of your greeting reached my ears, the baby in my womb leaped for joy. Blessed is she who has believed that the Lord would fulfill his promises to her!"
Luke 1:39-45

One of the great joys of being a dad was getting to interact with my children while they were in Grace's womb.

As they developed almost to full term, they would move so much and even respond to my voice.

Some family members told us that babies can hear and respond to our voices, so I would talk to my babies and read Scripture to them. There was so much joy and anticipation during this time.

I love the joy that children and newborns bring into our lives.

There was a supernatural joy event that took place around the incarnation of Jesus.

Elizabeth and Zechariah were the parents of John the Baptist, who would become the forerunner of Jesus.

Elizabeth was barren and God opened her womb miraculously.

She was carrying her child shortly before Mary became pregnant by the Holy Spirit with the Christ child. As relatives, they met when Mary went to Judea.

As soon as these two pregnant cousins met and Elizabeth heard Mary's voice, John leaped in Elizabeth's womb.

Mary was filled with the Holy Spirit and even baby John leaped for joy in this Holy Spirit encounter.

This fulfilled the angel's prophecy to Zechariah that John would be filled with the Spirit from his mother's womb.

Elizabeth had a revelation that Jesus was the Lord even while being carried by His mother Mary.

The Holy Spirit comes upon the revelation of the Lordship of Jesus.

The incarnation of Jesus ushered in the manifest Presence of God.

Remember, the Presence is the Person of God and His glory shines in the face of Jesus.

This Child was and is fully God and fully Man.

When He is near, there is supernatural joy, a revelation of who He is, and people are filled with the Holy Spirit.

The key to joy is to get near Jesus, to be in His Presence, and to be near those who carry the Presence of Christ.

There is a joy that comes from knowing who Jesus is and spending time with Him.

What a joy that God has become Man!

What a joy that we can receive the Spirit of God!

What a joy that comes from being near Him!

May You experience the joy of Jesus's nearness this Christmas.

Lord Jesus, how I love to be near You! There is joy in Your Presence! Let me marvel at the power of Your incarnation and the reality that You have entered our world so we could know You. Reveal Yourself to me and fill me afresh with Your Holy Spirit. Wash sadness away and let me live in Your joy. In Your name, amen.

Magnificat
December 17

And Mary said: "My soul glorifies the Lord and my spirit rejoices in God my Savior, for he has been mindful of the humble state of his servant. From now on all generations will call me blessed, for the Mighty One has done great things for me— holy is his name. His mercy extends to those who fear him, from generation to generation. He has performed mighty deeds with his arm; he has scattered those who are proud in their inmost thoughts. He has brought down rulers from their thrones but has lifted up the humble. He has filled the hungry with good things but has sent the rich away empty. He has helped his servant Israel, remembering to be merciful to Abraham and his descendants forever, just as he promised our ancestors."
Luke 1:46-55

Do you have a go to song of praise and a song of resistance? I notice a lot of athletes like to listen to the same song or playlist before they compete.

Music and songs have a way of inspiring us.

Being caught up in wonder through sounds and lyrics can compel our souls to believe for great things. This is why competitors bring their hearts and minds to a place of inspiration so they can move forward to see their desired outcomes.

This passage in Luke is Mary's song and known throughout church history as the *Magnificat* which means magnifies in Latin.

Mary magnified the Lord, overflowing with joy at the goodness of God after leaving Elizabeth's house with a Holy Spirit encounter.

God had chosen little humble Mary from a small town to be the mother of His Son, the Messiah.

History would be changed for all, but history was also changed for Mary. It was personal for her. God entrusted His eternal purposes to her.

Mary's song is filled with awe and praise to God, but it's also a prophecy about how the humble and hungry will receive from God, but the proud and earthly powerful will come under judgment.

It's a proclamation that the incarnation of Jesus would be God's undoing of evil and corruption in this world.

The Presence is always personal, but Jesus coming among us also had apocalyptic implications for the world.

This song gives us meaning in the midst of dark times and brings inspiration and joy when the stakes are high.

Mary would need a song for all that her heart would endure, as her Son was to suffer.

We need a song of Christ's victory in our heart to give us endurance and strength when we face opposition.

He is with us, and the order of everything has changed.

Magnify His name!

Father God, I magnify Your holy name! You see me and know me. Use me for Your purposes. Let me sing a song of victory for You have lifted up the humble and taken down the proud. You are worthy, Lord! In Jesus' name, amen.

HE HAS COME
DECEMBER 18

His father Zechariah was filled with the Holy Spirit and prophesied: "Praise be to the Lord, the God of Israel, because he has come to his people and redeemed them. He has raised up a horn of salvation for us in the house of his servant David (as he said through his holy prophets of long ago), salvation from our enemies and from the hand of all who hate us— to show mercy to our ancestors and to remember his holy covenant, the oath he swore to our father Abraham: to rescue us from the hand of our enemies, and to enable us to serve him without fear in holiness and righteousness before him all our days.
Luke 1:67-75

What is the thing you've waited the longest for?
Turning 18?
Or 21?
Moving out of your house?
Getting married?
Graduating high school or college?

Has there ever been a date or an event that you have waited with great anticipation for?

I think what I have waited for the longest is graduating with a graduate degree.

It's a lot of work so it's taking me longer than I estimated.

I was married relatively young, and we had children quickly. So, I don't feel like I have waited a long time for a lot of things.

But could you imagine waiting for something which your ancestors waited for, and took thousands of years to come?

Zechariah, the dad of John the Baptist, was struck mute because he didn't believe an angel who brought news that Elizabeth, his wife, who was barren, would have a child.

Zechariah was a priest and a faithful man, but he could not believe the child he waited for would come.

He had waited all his life for a child, and the people of Israel had waited thousands of years for their Messiah.

When John was born, Zechariah was finally able to speak. His first words were praise to God. He sang a song that is about Jesus and about the destiny of his son as the forerunner of the Messiah.

Before Zechariah begins to sing about Jesus, we learn that he, like his wife and son, is also filled with the Holy Spirit.

Every believer ought to prioritize the Spirit-filled life.

This is how God does His great work through ordinary people.

He was a man filled with the Presence.

And what does He sing about first? The Lord God of Israel had "come to His people."

This is all about the Presence.

Because Jesus came, the people would be redeemed.

Because Jesus came, they would be saved from their enemies.

In Jesus' coming, God's promise to Abraham was fulfilled.

In Jesus' coming, God's fulfillment of His promise to David was accomplished.

The promise of holiness and righteousness was fulfilled in Jesus.

Because He came, we can serve Him without fear.

Jesus has come.

Zechariah sang about it.

The wait was over, the promise was fulfilled.
Let us sing about Him forever and ever.
He has come! He is worthy!

Lord Jesus, You have come! You are worthy to be praised! You fulfilled the promises to Abraham and David. You will surely fulfill Your promises to me. I get to serve You without fear in righteousness and holiness. Be near to me, Lord Jesus. I love Your Presence. In Your name, amen.

Peace on Earth
December 19

And there were in the same country shepherds abiding in the field, keeping watch over their flock by night. And, lo, the angel of the Lord came upon them, and the glory of the Lord shone round about them: and they were sore afraid. And the angel said unto them, Fear not: for, behold, I bring you good tidings of great joy, which shall be to all people. For unto you is born this day in the city of David a Saviour, which is Christ the Lord. And this shall be a sign unto you; Ye shall find the babe wrapped in swaddling clothes, lying in a manger. And suddenly there was with the angel a multitude of the heavenly host praising God, and saying, Glory to God in the highest, And on earth peace, good will toward men.
Luke 2:8-14 KJV

Have you ever been minding your own business and suddenly something incredible happens that you weren't expecting?

In the days before I had a cell phone, I was sitting at home one day, and a friend called me.

He was at a local music store and said I had to get there right away because a world-famous drummer was there giving a clinic.

I decided to spontaneously leave the house, and I was so glad I did.

This drummer put on a clinic all right.

As a musician, I had never seen such artistry.

I was blown away by the talent and music.

I almost missed out on something great, because sometimes the greatest things that happen aren't planned.

When Jesus was born, there was a group of shepherds nearby in a field, and an angel appeared to them along with the glory of the Lord.

When the Presence came upon them, they were afraid, and the angel had to tell them to "fear not."

Sometimes people are so casual and even flippant as they share about their encounters with angels and God's Presence, but in the Bible, people are usually afraid and told to fear not, because of the greatness of God's glory.

These shepherds were minding their own business.

They didn't know their regular life was going to be interrupted with the greatest opportunity anyone could ask for in history; to see Jesus as a newborn baby.

The angel announced that he brought great news of great joy. He said there was a sign that they would find Jesus lying in a manger.

Greater than the sign of the angels was a sign of the baby. The Presence had come in the Person of Christ.

God was here to save the day.

Of course, this sign was accompanied by the sign of the angel and then a great company of angels also started singing "Glory to God in the highest, and on earth peace, goodwill toward men."

Is there a greater praise than declaring "Glory to God in the highest?"

Oh, He deserves the highest praise that He would send His Son for us to be born as us.

This meant there was now peace on the earth.

The Presence of Jesus means peace on the earth and goodwill or favor for humanity.

Our greatest need is peace.

Jesus brings us into peace with God and makes us to live in peace with one another.

His peace is stronger than war and hatred.

When He is here and near, all that causes chaos, violence, division and war is defeated by His peace.

When He returns, His peace will triumph over all other enemies and will last forever.

He has come and He will come again; there will be peace on the earth forever.

Come, Lord Jesus.

―――

Lord Jesus, Prince of Peace, I worship You! Glory to God in the highest and on earth peace, goodwill toward men! Let me walk in holy fear that I might reverence Your name. Let me walk in great joy for the great news that Christ has come and will come again. Let me join in the praise of angels. I love You, my Lord. In Your name, amen.

Dedicated
December 20

When the time came for the purification rites required by the Law of Moses, Joseph and Mary took him to Jerusalem to present him to the Lord (as it is written in the Law of the Lord, "Every firstborn male is to be consecrated to the Lord"), and to offer a sacrifice in keeping with what is said in the Law of the Lord: "a pair of doves or two young pigeons."
Luke 2:22-24

Have you been to a child dedication in the church?
One of the favorite things for Grace and I, as pastors, is dedicating children unto the Lord.
It is a holy thing for parents to bring their babies before the church and set them apart to the Lord in prayer so they might be consecrated unto God's purposes.

We dedicated our four children to the Lord.

Our church tradition is to sing the classic *Jesus Love Me* song over the children we dedicate.

When Jesus was first born, Mary and Joseph took Jesus to the temple to present Him, or dedicate Him, to the Lord. The Lord was being dedicated unto the Lord.

The incarnation is such a wonder to marvel over.

God in the flesh going to God's house to be consecrated unto God.

Jesus was fully human while being fully God. As our representative, He perfectly fulfilled the law of God for us, so we could be consecrated and set apart unto the Lord.

Child dedication is not a mere ritual, but is also the pattern of our Lord Jesus.

When someone or something is set apart unto God, it is holy.

The Presence of God comes upon people and things offered unto the Lord.

Our sacrifices and dedications touch the Lord's heart and He is pleased with our obedience to put Him first.

Setting ourselves and our child apart to Him is about putting Him first and reminding ourselves that we are not our own, we belong to Him.

Jesus' life was God's gift to us, and His life being set apart unto God was also His gift back to the Father.

If you have children, or you will have children, dedicate them to the Lord. Follow the example of Jesus.

This Christmas when you exchange gifts, remember you can give God a gift.

The greatest gift we bring God is ourselves.

Jesus came to offer His life for our redemption.

Our response to yield to Him and honor His coming and sacrifice for us touches His heart like nothing else. The offering of our livers as worship was the purpose we were made for, and brings us joy as we bring it to Him.

———

Lord Jesus, I love You! I dedicate and offer my life to You. I present myself to You so that I might live in Your Presence. There is none like You! You are worthy of my life. My life is not my own. Be first in my life, Lord. I give You the highest place. In Your name, amen.

Moved by the Spirit
December 21

Now there was a man in Jerusalem called Simeon, who was righteous and devout. He was waiting for the consolation of Israel, and the Holy Spirit was on him. It had been revealed to him by the Holy Spirit that he would not die before he had seen the Lord's Messiah. Moved by the Spirit, he went into the temple courts. When the parents brought in the child Jesus to do for him what the custom of the Law required, Simeon took him in his arms and praised God, saying: "Sovereign Lord, as you have promised, you may now dismiss your servant in peace. For my eyes have seen your salvation, which you have prepared in the sight of all nations: a light for revelation to the Gentiles, and the glory of your people Israel." The child's father and mother marveled at what was said about him. Then Simeon blessed them and said to Mary, his mother: "This child is destined to cause the falling and rising of many in Israel, and to be a sign that will be spoken against, so that the thoughts of many hearts will be revealed. And a sword will pierce your own soul too."
Luke 2:25-35

Have you ever sat with an older man of God in His later years? I've been blessed to have men in their senior years pour into me, like Dr. Matthew Thomas and Dr. Stephen List.

There is a great anointing and stability on men who have gone the distance in ministry and faithfulness to Jesus. The Presence of God increases through the crushing, maturity, and resilience of people who go through many trials and never give up on loving and following Jesus.

I think that often, people give up too early, not realizing that the greatest things happen for people who wait a very long time for them.

I receive so much encouragement and strength sitting with these men of God. They are men moved by the Holy Spirit.

There is a man who Scripture doesn't say a lot about around the birth of Jesus, named Simeon.

But what it says about this righteous and devout man is powerful. He was a man who the Holy Spirit was upon, who had things revealed to him by the Holy Spirit, and who was moved by the Holy Spirit.

He was a Presence man.

His whole life was saturated with and compelled by the Spirit.

He was prophetic and his life promise was to see the Messiah.

He waited for God with us.

He waited for the manifestation of the Presence among us.

He prophesied out of his rich fellowship with the Holy Spirit.

He prophesied that the coming of Jesus would pierce the soul of Mary.

Those who want to be close to Jesus will see great wonders, but will also see their souls pierced with grief. For the coming of Jesus meant that one day, He would die for us.

If we want our lives to find true significance, we have so much to learn from Simeon.

Be a man or woman of the Holy Spirit.

Spend time in God's house and in God's Presence, to hear God's voice and know prophetically what season in which we live.

Don't give up, but be willing to wait for God's promises in your life.

And ultimately, find your significance not in your own story, but find your meaning in the center of Jesus' story.

Lord Jesus, light to the Gentiles and the glory of Israel, be in the center of my life. May my life find meaning in Your story. I want to live for You as a child of God, who the Holy Spirit is upon, who the Holy Spirit reveals things to, and who is moved by the Holy Spirit. In Your name Jesus, amen.

Hidden Heroes
December 22

There was also a prophet, Anna, the daughter of Penuel, of the tribe of Asher. She was very old; she had lived with her husband seven years after her marriage, and then was a widow until she was eighty-four. She never left the temple but worshiped night and day, fasting and praying. Coming up to them at that very moment, she gave thanks to God and spoke about the child to all who were looking forward to the redemption of Jerusalem.
Luke 2:36-38

Do you have any hidden heroes in your life?

You know, people you look up to that could go unnoticed, but make a huge impact all around them.

I'm talking about the type of people who don't carry titles or earthly fame, but they know how to move heaven and earth in prayer.

Monel Benson and Norma Bass are two women that devoted much of their lives to prayer in our church when I was growing up. They carried the Presence and boy, could they pray.

If you were in trouble, you wanted them to pray for you; and if you were causing trouble, you wanted to stay away, because they also carried the fear of the Lord.

When baby Jesus came to the temple for his dedication to the Lord, there was another older saint, a widow named Anna, who had waited for the Messiah to be born.

She spent her years at the temple in prayer, worship, and fasting. Her life exemplified that to waste your life on the Lord is not a waste at all.

Anna's life found significance around the Presence of Jesus.

Prayer is simple enough to do, but we can be so preoccupied with other things in life.

People often want to be important, but it is actually a life of prayer and ministry to the Lord with Jesus at the center that creates eternal impact.

It's simple to be a person of the Presence. It comes down to prioritizing ministering to our Lord above anything else.

Out of her prayer life, Anna proclaims who Jesus is to all who will hear.

Those who are most in love become the greatest preachers. The hidden commitment of love and devotion to Jesus spills out into a public love.

Thank God for the fiery widows like Anna.

We are blessed to have several in our church.

Through the ages, many widows, monks and contemplative souls became examples for us about what is possible when one centers their life around ministry to the Lord.

The greatest gift we can give our Lord, as believers, is our time and attention in adoration that flows by His grace into obedience.

———

Lord Jesus, be the center of my life. My meaning is found in You. I can so easily stray from the simplicity of prayer and worship. I want my life to be full of adoration and devotion. I want everyone to know of my love for You. In Your holy name, amen.

Wise Men
December 23

After Jesus was born in Bethlehem in Judea, during the time of King Herod, Magi from the east came to Jerusalem and asked, "Where is the one who has been born king of the Jews? We saw his star when it rose and have come to worship him."
Matthew 2:1-2

Have you ever given lavish gifts to someone?

I don't know if I have ever given a lavish or overly costly gift to anyone, other than the wedding ring I bought my wife.

But I love to give Grace gifts that have meaning and that bring her joy. I love to give her more than she is expecting.

I usually stretch or outright break my budget when I shop for her Christmas gifts. She does so much for us, so I love getting to bless her and give her things that show her how much I honor her.

There are some important figures that show up in the Christmas story, but are often misplaced and misrepresented.

They are the wise men or magi from the east.

People often think there were three of them because they gave gold, frankincense and myrrh.

But where the Bible records their three gifts, it does not record how many actual magi there were who visited Jesus.

The nativity sets people display in their home or yard often show the wise men with shepherds, but the wise men did not get to visit Jesus until He was about two years old.

The magi were kind of like astrologers who looked to the stars for guidance, and when they saw a star from the east, they knew God was reaching out to them to reveal that Jesus, the King of the Jews, was born.

They followed the star because they wanted to worship Jesus.

God had to supernaturally direct them, because King Herod was jealous and ordered that all two-year-old Jewish boys and younger be executed.

God reveals Jesus to people from the nations, from poverty, blue collar work, to spiritual magi and the financially affluent.

The question we have to ask ourselves is, will we forsake what we know and go on a long journey, as the magi did, to follow Jesus?

Will we forsake what we know and are comfortable with to find our joy in encountering Jesus?

In the Presence of Jesus, the magi found joy, worshipped and gave extravagant gifts.

Our worship ought to be the same.

We should give Jesus our best because nothing is better than Him.

As the saying goes, "Wise men still seek Him."

May we be those who seek His Presence and prize Him above all else.

Lord Jesus, I bring You my worship. Let my love and honor be lavish for You. I give You my best. There is no one or nothing else greater than You. I love You with all my heart. You bring me joy! I bow before You and adore You. In Your precious name, amen.

CHRISTMAS EVE
DECEMBER 24

So Joseph also went up from the town of Nazareth in Galilee to Judea, to Bethlehem the town of David, because he belonged to the house and line of David. He went there to register with Mary, who was pledged to be married to him and was expecting a child. While they were there, the time came for the baby to be born,
Luke 2:4-6

When you were growing up, was it hard for you to sleep on Christmas Eve?

I had a hard time falling asleep on Christmas Eve. I was so excited.

It's the same for our children.

There is so much anticipation of gifts on Christmas morning.

To be so close to Christmas but still have to wait feels like torture for most children.

I wonder how often in life we don't realize how close we are to God manifesting in a great way.

Of course, Mary and Joseph knew Mary could give birth soon, but the world was about to change and barely anyone knew what was taking place.

Mary and Joseph were just one day away from the greatest event in human history. The prophecies of old were finally about to be fulfilled and the wait would be over.

The Messiah was about to be born.

When the Presence of God doesn't seem to manifest and you are waiting for Him to show up in your life, just wait a little longer. He's about to show up.

Mary and Joseph were going about their normal business to register for the census. They didn't know that their obedience to mundane government orders was setting them up to fulfill prophecy about where the Messiah was born.

God gets us where we need to be for His Presence and work to manifest in our lives.

He can show up anywhere and anytime.

He accomplishes His purposes in our lives when we are often unaware.

I think people count God out at times, when they are just one day away from a breakthrough.

Don't try to discern God's will by how spiritual you feel or how great your surroundings are.

Don't count God out while you are waiting for His promise.

Don't measure your spirituality by how much you feel God's Presence.

Obey Him in the small things and keep a posture of trust.

One more day and everything can change.

———

Lord Jesus, sometimes I am going through the motions of life, and I fail to recognize how you are about to manifest. Let me be aware of Your Presence. Let me not give up or lose heart when I am waiting for You. You are worth the wait. In Your name, amen.

Christmas Day
December 25

And she gave birth to her firstborn, a son. She wrapped him in cloths and placed him in a manger, because there was no guest room available for them.
Luke 2:7

What brings you the most joy on Christmas morning?

For me, it's time alone with my wife and children.

Grace and I especially love getting to bless our children with gifts and watch their reaction as they open presents. Each year gets more precious as they grow up.

I think I enjoy it more each year because I realize the season with them could change soon as they get older.

I also just love thinking more deeply about what Jesus has done in His incarnation.

One thing is for sure, I love the feeling of Christmas morning after all the work, hustle and bustle, shopping, Christmas parties, and special church services.

It all leads up to the reminder that Jesus came.

He is here for us.

I can be present and remember the Presence of the One who changed everything.

When Mary gave birth to Jesus, there was no room for them, so they had to stay near a manger, a place for animals on the side of a house.

But He was here, God with us, Immanuel.

He was here, the light in the darkness.

He was here, the fulfillment of the prophets.

The waiting was over.

The Messiah had arrived.

I love what Maximus the Confessor said about the incarnation, "If he has brought to completion his mystical work of becoming human, having become like us in every way save without sin (cf Heb 4115), and even descended into the lower regions of the earth where the tyranny of sin compelled humanity, then God will also completely fulfill the goal of his mystical work of deifying humanity in every respect, of course, short of an identity of essence with God; and he will assimilate humanity to himself and elevate us to a position above all the heavens. It is to this exalted position that the natural magnitude of God's grace summons lowly humanity, out of a goodness that is infinite ." *

Jesus had accomplished God's plan of humbling himself from heaven to earth so that He might elevate us from earth to heaven.

This humble birth, the Presence of the King as a newborn baby, is hard to fathom in all its implications.

St. Athanasius in his incredible work, *On the Incarnation*, gets to the end of His work and seems almost speechless at all that he has studied and written. Near the end of his work he says "And, in a word, the achievements of the Saviour, resulting from His becoming man, are of such kind and number, that if one should wish to enumerate them, he may be compared to men who gaze at the expanse of the sea and wish to count its waves. For as one cannot take in the whole of the waves with his eyes, for those which are coming on baffle the sense of him that attempts it; so for him that would take in all the achievements of Christ in the body, it is impossible to take in the whole, even by reckoning them up, as those which go beyond his thought are more than those he

thinks he has taken in. Better is it, then, not to aim at speaking of the whole, where one cannot do justice even to a part, but, after mentioning one more, to leave the whole for you to marvel at. For all alike are marvellous, and wherever a man turns his glance, he may behold on that side the divinity of the Word, and be struck with exceeding great awe."
**

>He came to us.
>We didn't make our way to Him.
>He changed everything.
>May we live in awe and wonder of all He has done.

Lord Jesus, King of glory, God of God and Light of Light, the One who holds all things but was born in a manger, the One who has shown us that greatness is found in humility, I marvel at Your incarnation. You have come to me. May I never lose the wonder of all You have done to become Man that I might know You and be exalted to eternal life with You forever. In Your most precious name, amen.

In the Same Way
December 26

After he said this, he was taken up before their very eyes, and a cloud hid him from their sight. They were looking intently up into the sky as he was going, when suddenly two men dressed in white stood beside them. "Men of Galilee," they said, "why do you stand here looking into the sky? This same Jesus, who has been taken from you into heaven, will come back in the same way you have seen him go into heaven."
Acts 1:9-11

Do you like the day after Christmas?
What do you think about it?
Are you sad Christmas is over?
Are you thankful?
Or a bit of both?

I love the day after Christmas because it means I have time off with my family and we rarely have to be anywhere after such a busy month.

As I learn more of the incarnation, the more I want to focus on not just that He has come, but that He is coming again.

May the last week of our year be fixed on the word Maranatha, "The

Lord has come, or come Lord." Yes, Christmas is over this year, and we remember He has come, but He is coming again.

I can't think of a better way to prepare for the new year than to think of the new world that will come about when Jesus returns.

Whatever will prepare us for His coming again will prepare us for another year.

When the apostles who had walked with Jesus and got to know Him so intimately saw the post-resurrected Jesus, their lives were changed.

He spent forty days teaching them from the Scriptures about Himself and the kingdom of God.

But the time came for Him to leave and send us the Helper so that we might finish the work of Jesus across the world of preaching the gospel and making disciples.

Angels appeared to the disciples as Jesus ascended into heaven, assuring them of His return.

He has come, and He is coming again.

He will be with us forever.

Not only by faith through the Spirit now, but by sight.

If you think we experience the Presence now, just wait until He comes back. He isn't coming as a baby next time; He is coming in the sky, victorious and glorious.

"And you will also learn about His second glorious and truly divine appearing to us, when no longer in lowliness, but in His own glory—no longer in humble guise, but in His own magnificence—He is to come, no more to suffer, but thenceforth to render to all the fruit of His own Cross, that is, the resurrection and incorruption; and no longer to be judged, but to judge all, by what each has done in the body, whether good or evil; where there is laid up for the good the kingdom of heaven, but for them that have done evil everlasting fire and outer darkness ." *

Oh, what a day that will be when He returns on the clouds.

We cry Maranatha Lord! How we long for Your Presence. How we long for You to be with us forever.

If your life is not ready for His return, repent and make Jesus the Lord of your life. It's too late to wait until He comes back in the sky. Now is your chance to give your heart and your life.

Lord Jesus, King of glory. You have come and You will come again. Let my life be prepared for Your return in power and glory. As I remember You came, may I live with urgency that You will come again. Cleanse me of sin and disobedience. You gave everything for me in Your incarnation, death, and resurrection. I believe in You, Son of God. I give You my life. In Your name, amen.

Present You

December 27

To him who is able to keep you from stumbling and to present you before his glorious Presence without fault and with great joy— to the only God our Savior be glory, majesty, power and authority, through Jesus Christ our Lord, before all ages, now and forevermore! Amen.
Jude 1:24-25

Have you ever tried to hold on to something so hard, then you lose it?

Was it a relationship, a goal or a career opportunity that you pursued with all of your heart?

I don't have anything major on my mind at the moment, but I know there have been many instances when I wanted something so badly, and as I tried to make things happen, they just wouldn't work out.

Sometimes we hold so firmly to something, but it just ends up draining us from all the effort and it's not really something God had for us.

The good news about our relationship with God is that it's not about our effort to hold on to God, but about His ability to hold on to us.

Life in the Presence is not about what we pursue, but the reality and invitation we respond to by the grace of God. He pursues us and only in response to His pursuit may we pursue Him.

At the conclusion of the short book of Jude, we are reminded about our life in the Presence not being about our effort alone or our effort primarily.

Jude says that the "glory, majesty, power and authority" are through Jesus who is "able to keep you from stumbling."

Not only does He keep us from stumbling, but He will also one day "present you before His glorious Presence without fault and great joy."

Jesus is active now in our Christian walk to keep us from stumbling and is active in the future to present us in His glorious Presence.

What a marvelous truth that Jesus looks forward to presenting us without fault and with great joy!

Jesus takes joy over us being with Him forever, free and clean in His Presence.

He is present with us now through the Spirit, but there is a day where we will live in His full, immediate, and unhindered glory.

The One who was present before the ages began will join us to Himself for the ages forevermore!

This life in the Presence is about God's ability to call us to Himself, His ability to keep us, and His ability and promise to present us before His Presence in the age to come.

Our time with Him is a response and yielding to the great work of His grace and active Presence in our lives.

Jesus Christ our Lord delights in us.

Enter into the Presence of His joy and His delight.

Lord Jesus, my love for You is a response to Your great loving pursuit of my life. You have been present to empower me and help me overcome my stumbling, and one day You will present me faultless with great joy! How I long for that day where I spend eternity in the fullness of Your glory. In Your great name, the only God our Savior, be glory, majesty, power and authority, Jesus Christ my Lord, before all ages, now and forevermore amen!

Throne Room Mission
December 28

Then I saw a Lamb, looking as if it had been slain, standing at the center of the throne, encircled by the four living creatures and the elders. The Lamb had seven horns and seven eyes, which are the seven spirits of God sent out into all the earth. He went and took the scroll from the right hand of him who sat on the throne. And when he had taken it, the four living creatures and the twenty-four elders fell down before the Lamb. Each one had a harp and they were holding golden bowls full of incense, which are the prayers of God's people. And they sang a new song, saying: "You are worthy to take the scroll and to open its seals, because you were slain, and with your blood you purchased for God persons from every tribe and language and people and nation. You have made them to be a kingdom and priests to serve our God, and they will reign on the earth."
Revelation 5:6-10

What is the longest prayer meeting you have attended?

I've been part of 48 hour prayer meetings, weeks of prayer and fasting, and all-night prayer meetings.

Have you heard the story of Count Ludwig Von Zinzendorf and the Moravians?

Zinzendorf was a wealthy landowner and brought unity to various Christian groups who came as immigrants. They organized a prayer meeting that lasted twenty-four hours a day for 100 years.

The Moravians launched the greatest missions movement at that time in history. They had a profound impact, as they influenced John Wesley and what would become the Methodist movement and churches.

There are stories of Moravian missionaries who sold themselves into slavery because it was the only way they could get to some nations that they felt a burden for.

I've heard accounts of Moravians who were on ships leaving their port who would cry out to those bidding them farewell on the docks, "To win for the Lamb that was slain the rewards of His suffering."

Their devotion to the Presence in prayer fueled a love for Jesus that compelled them to spread the gospel to the nations.

When you are in the Presence, God shares His heart with you and His heart is for the nations.

But when we get His heart for people and we go to the nations to win them to Jesus, they become a part of the company of saints that worship Jesus forever.

Presence motivates mission for the right reasons: pure love.

But missions end is Presence.

In Revelation 5, John sees the extravagant worship around the throne of the slain and risen Lamb, Jesus Christ. He hears that Jesus has redeemed by His blood those from every tribe, language, people, and nation.

Jesus will be worshiped forever by every ethnic and language group on the planet.

When unreached people groups receive a witness in their own

language of the gospel, receive a Bible in their language and surrender to our Lord, Revelation 5 is still being fulfilled in our day.

Just imagine that Jesus is still longing to hear His name praised from languages that have never uttered His name.

The price of missions is a privilege, as believers sacrifice time in prayer, finances and their very lives so that Jesus will receive glory forever from all peoples and tribes.

Jesus loves the nations, and He is worthy to be worshiped in all languages.

May His Presence fuel us in mission and may our mission help fill heaven with all languages for His glory.

———

King Jesus, Lamb of God who was slain before the foundation of the world, let my life bring You glory. May Your church and I win for You the rewards of Your suffering. I ask You to share Your heart with me for the nations. You are worthy of worship forever from every tribe, language, people, and nation. In Your great name, amen.

The Rider on the White Horse
December 29

I saw heaven standing open and there before me was a white horse, whose rider is called Faithful and True. With justice he judges and wages war. His eyes are like blazing fire, and on his head are many crowns. He has a name written on him that no one knows but he himself. He is dressed in a robe dipped in blood, and his name is the Word of God. The armies of heaven were following him, riding on white horses and dressed in fine linen, white and clean. Coming out of his mouth is a sharp sword with which to strike down the nations. "He will rule them with an iron scepter." He treads the winepress of the fury of the wrath of God Almighty. On his robe and on his thigh he has this name written: king of kings and Lord of Lords.
Revelation 19:11-16

Have you ever heard a friend go on and on about someone before, even saying that you just have to meet this person?

Then it can become a situation where this person you have heard so much about has legend-like status in your mind.

Sometimes we do this with celebrities or famous athletes.

When John gets towards the end of Revelation, He tells us not about a living legend, but about the living King Jesus Christ and His return.

Think about this moment in the future when Jesus comes back on a white horse. He is the One we have heard about our whole lives, the One we read about in the Scriptures, and we will no longer wonder what it will be like to meet Him, but we will see Him.

I realize this is only for the last generation who gets to live for His return.

What a day that will be!

What John describes fills my heart to awe and holy fear.

My King is coming back on a white horse. His name is faithful and true. His eyes are like fire. He is leading a heavenly army to victory. He will make all wrong things right.

For me it's a day to look forward to in wonder and astonishment.

For those who oppose our Jesus and resist Him, it will be a terrible day of judgement.

The Presence of Jesus bodily on the earth again will mean judgment and removal of all evil, sin and ultimately death. He will allow nothing sinful or wrong to remain.

He will not come back as an innocent baby but as the glorious Ruler and Judge triumphing over all His enemies.

His immediate Presence on the earth again will mean that His kingdom has fully come and His will as the King of kings and Lord of lords will be done.

This day of His return brings His judgment, but also the glorious future of humanity who have received Jesus as Lord.

I urge anyone who has not received Jesus as Lord to do so before it's too late upon His return to judge and rule the nations.

My Jesus, King of kings and Lord of lords, let my heart stay ready for Your return on judgment day. I am thrilled to see You again upon the earth, the One my heart loves and fears who is called Faithful and True. There is no one like You! You are worthy of my whole life! I ask that You help me live in preparation for the day You come. In Your mighty name, Jesus, amen.

Eternal Dwelling
December 30

And I heard a loud voice from the throne saying, "Look! God's dwelling place is now among the people, and he will dwell with them. They will be his people, and God himself will be with them and be their God. 'He will wipe every tear from their eyes. There will be no more death' or mourning or crying or pain, for the old order of things has passed away..." He said to me: "It is done. I am the Alpha and the Omega, the Beginning and the End. To the thirsty I will give water without cost from the spring of the water of life. Those who are victorious will inherit all this, and I will be their God and they will be my children. But the cowardly, the unbelieving, the vile, the murderers, the sexually immoral, those who practice magic arts, the idolaters and all liars—they will be consigned to the fiery lake of burning sulfur. This is the second death..." I did not see a temple in the city, because the Lord God Almighty and the Lamb are its temple. The city does not need the sun or the moon to shine on it, for the glory of God gives it light, and the Lamb is its lamp.
Revelation 21:3-4, 6-8, 22-23

Have you experienced that feeling of such intense fun with friends that you wished it could last forever?

I've had times growing up and times with my own family now that feels like the best of times, where everyone is talking, sharing, laughing and eating together.

It's in those times that I don't want our time together to end.

The night becomes late, people fall asleep, and everyone has to retire to their own rooms or go back to their homes.

There is a longing for these times of fellowship and joy to go on continually.

This is like the longing for the eternal Presence.

As John continues to share the climax of His visions in Revelation, he says that after the return of Jesus and the final judgement, God speaks from His throne that His dwelling place is now among the people.

The Presence will be eternal and unending for all the redeemed who are victorious. We are God's people, and He is our God. He will be with us, and we will be with Him. Nothing else matters in the end than being with our God forever.

The Lord Almighty and the Lamb, Jesus Christ will be our temple forever.

The story of God's Presence in Eden, manifested in Moses's and David's Tabernacle, manifested in Solomon's Temple, manifested in the church and in each believer, will now be measureless and unhindered forever in the immediate Presence of our God.

Everything we have experienced since Eden that has been lost will be fully restored. The story began with Adam and Eve dwelling with God in a garden and now Revelation 20-22 says we will dwell with God in a garden forever.

God Himself becomes our light, our warmth, our Temple.

Our surrender to Jesus in this life matters for eternity.

The inheritance of the wicked who practice sin, idolatry, and immorality is destruction.

But the inheritance of the righteous who receive from Jesus the water of life have the inheritance of the Presence, getting to dwell with God.

Our future inheritance as believers is the restoration of Eden and not only the restoration of the temples throughout Israel and the church's history, but the ultimate fulfillment of God Himself being our Temple, where we encounter the Presence together forever.

Lord Jesus, thank You for taking my place on the cross and giving me new life. I ask for boldness to live for You and be prepared for the day where I will meet You face to face. You are the eternal longing of my soul. You are my temple, my dwelling place and my eternal inheritance. Let me live in urgency for this day and tell others of the greatness of Your plan to welcome us all into Your Presence forever. In Your great and glorious name, my Lord Jesus Christ, amen.

Maranatha

December 31

The Spirit and the bride say, "Come!" And let the one who hears say, "Come!" Let the one who is thirsty come; and let the one who wishes take the free gift of the water of life... He who testifies to these things says, "Yes, I am coming soon." Amen. Come, Lord Jesus.
Revelation 22:17, 20

What is the greatest invitation you have ever received?

How did you feel when you received it?

Have you ever been a VIP? A truly very important person at an event?

What made you feel so special about being a special guest?

Of course, the greatest invitation I have ever received was to be invited into this life-changing love relationship with Jesus.

The greatest invitation I ever gave was asking my wife to marry me.

All of us were made for love and attention.

Our fallenness has allowed our desire for attention to become twisted and selfish, but we were made for love and attention.

To never have someone invite us or show us affection would cause damage to our souls.

An invitation reveals desire and conveys love because an invitation says I see you and I want to spend time with you.

Our relationship with Jesus, this fellowship with the Presence, has only occurred because of God creating us, inviting us and making the way for us through His sacrifice.

But we also see in the Scripture that where God takes divine initiative and gives us an invitation to really know Him, He is looking for a human response.

We are not the only ones who desire to be seen and known.

There is nothing missing in God that we can add to Him, but there is a longing in His heart for fellowship and friendship.

There is a longing in His heart to share His love with us and for us to know One another.

There is a longing in our Savior for His bride, the church.

At the end of Revelation and the end of the whole Bible, we hear one last time the Maranatha cry, "Come Lord."

Our Lord Jesus Himself says, "The Spirit and the bride say come!"

The Spirit and the bride are crying out for Jesus to come back.

We along with the Spirit of God, are asking Him to come and be with us.

We are inviting our Lord to return for our great marriage to Him as the bride, His church. We are inviting our Lord to be with us now and to dwell with us forever.

But John doesn't stop there. He says there is another cry for him who hears this and that cry is "Let the one who is thirsty come."

There is living water, new life and a relationship with Jesus.

Our cry is for Jesus to come and be with us.

His cry is for all who realize they are thirsty without Him to come to Him as the source of life and be satisfied by His living water.

Jesus last words in the Bible are "Yes, I am coming soon."

He has promised His Presence and He will fulfill that urgency.

There is an ache in our hearts to be with the One we love both now and forever.

Our prayer to Jesus' last words is Maranatha, "Amen. Come, Lord Jesus."

Lord Jesus, the Bridegroom, the Root and the Offspring of David, the bright Morning Star, I join with the Spirit and the bride and cry out, "Come!" Maranatha, my precious Savior. I long for Your return. Come, Lord Jesus. Amen.

Bibliography

October 4th
https://heartcryforchange.com/team/rachel-hickson/

October 10th
https://bjm.org/

November 5th
Chesterton, G.K. *Orthodoxy*. John Lane, 1908.

November 7th
Coach Tim Notke is credited with saying, *"Hard work beats talent when talent doesn't work hard."* This quote has been widely circulated in sports and motivational contexts, though it gained greater popularity after being repeated by athletes like Kevin Durant.

November 10th
"Never Give In" Speech
Delivered by Winston Churchill at Harrow School on October 29, 1941.

November 19th
Chesterton, G.K. A Short History of England. London: Chatto & Windus, 1917.

November 21st
John Piper, The Sweetest Good of the Good News, quoting youth minister, Desiring-God.org, Feb. 2013.

November 25th
Quoted from a sermon by Pastor Mark Brattrud, Exact date and sermon title unknown. https://www.vcachurch.com/staff/

December 2nd
*"Jesus is God as if He was not human and Jesus is human as if He was not God at the same time without contradiction." —Bill Hogg
**Athanasius of Alexandria. On the Incarnation of the Word. Translated by Philip Schaff, in Nicene and Post-Nicene Fathers, Series 2, Vol. 4, edited by Philip Schaff and Henry Wace, Christian Classics Ethereal Library, https://www.ccel.org/ccel/athanasius/incarnation.

December 25th
*Maximus the Confessor. *On the Cosmic Mystery of Jesus Christ*. Translated by Paul M.

Blowers and Robert Louis Wilken. Crestwood, NY: St. Vladimir's Seminary Press, 2003.

** Athanasius of Alexandria. *On the Incarnation of the Word*. Translated by Archibald Robertson. In *Nicene and Post-Nicene Fathers*, Series II, Vol. 4. Edited by Philip Schaff and Henry Wace. Buffalo, NY: Christian Literature Publishing Co., 1892. Public domain. Accessed December 25th, 2023. https://ccel.org/ccel/athanasius/incarnation

December 26th

The Complete Works of St. Athanasius (20 Books): Cross-Linked to the Bible by Saint Athanasius

Also by John Hammer

eXXXit

The Presence Series:

- The Lord of the Presence
- The Power of the Presence
- The Pursuit of the Presence
- The Wonder of the Presence

Altars over Thrones

Contact

To continue to get more writing and updates from John or invite John to speak go subscribe to his Substack at johnandhammer.substack.com

About the Author

John Hammer is married to the love of his life Grace Elaine and Dad to four amazing children: Hailey, Emma, Justus and Addison. John is a graduate of Seattle Bible College. He loves communication through preaching, teaching, writing poetry and prose, as well as theological or philosophical conversations. He enjoys laughter at family dinners and staying active with them through Brazilian-Jiu Jitsu, Pickleball, and river walks. He and Grace are the Lead Pastors at Sonrise Christian Center in Everett, WA. He is also a co-founder of The Way and Represent Conferences. Johnandhammer.substack.com | isonrise.org

www.ingramcontent.com/pod-product-compliance
Lightning Source LLC
Chambersburg PA
CBHW020922090426
42736CB00010B/1005